SCIENTIFIC AND TECHNICAL EDUCATION IN NINETEENTH-CENTURY ENGLAND

SCIENTIFIC AND TECHNICAL EDUCATION IN NINETEENTH-CENTURY ENGLAND

A Symposium

by

Gordon W. Roderick
MA, BSc, PhD, MInstP

and

Michael D. Stephens
MA, MEd, PhD

DAVID & CHARLES : NEWTON ABBOT

ISBN 0 7153 5777 8

Set in 11 on 13pt Times New Roman
and printed in Great Britain by
Latimer Trend & Company Ltd Plymouth
for David & Charles (Holdings) Limited
South Devon House Newton Abbot Devon

Contents

Introduction

At mid-century Britain was riding the crest of the industrial wave and the quarter of a century following the repeal of the Corn Laws in 1846 has been called the Golden Age of British Capitalism. 'Politicians and economists waxed lyrical in their praise of the British economic system and the rest of the world was inclined to look at Great Britain as holding the keys to commercial prosperity . . . the typical Victorian of the Golden Age felt he could afford to be an optimist . . . The prosperity of the early 1870s looked as solid as the mahogany of Russell Square and there were few to foretell the troubles to come.'[1] But by 1870 the British economic achievement was already waning, the tide had turned and by 1900 a remarkable transformation had taken place. Britain had been the leader of the first Industrial Revolution and her success in this was based on the export of textiles, heavy machinery and iron goods. The industries of the second Industrial Revolution, however, were more science-based—organic chemicals, fertilisers and explosives, electrical engineering and steel—and Germany made rapid developments in these. The period 1870–90 was, according to Clapham, one in which 'Germany took the lead in Europe with speed and decision'.[2] But not only did Germany lay great emphasis on the more efficient production of new goods, she sought to win new markets in Europe, South America, China and India and as market after market fell to the Germans 'there were times, particularly towards 1900, when foreign competition seemed to be a brooding menace rather than a bracing challenge and the familiar label "Made in Germany" was used as the theme of the grimmest foreboding'.[3]

Britain's pre-eminence in the first Industrial Revolution had been founded on a combination of capital accumulation, natural mineral resources, the development of transport systems to establish internal and export trades, allied to an inventiveness which produced the few crucial breakthroughs and gave Britain an

7

overwhelming lead. On the other hand Britain's industrial success had little to do with her educational institutions. But at the beginning of the nineteenth century Germany embarked on a policy of creating a highly organised, technically trained society based on a State-aided national system of education. From an early date Germany developed a cohesive system of schools, universities and technical high schools which serviced industry and provided the manpower; and training at all levels, from apprentice to research-scientist, was generally superior. Germany's later industrial success, therefore, was seen as a reaping of the reward for her earlier investment in science and technical education.

No such development occurred in Britain and an integrated and co-ordinated school system was not established until the Education Act of 1902, which placed the responsibility for secondary education firmly in the hands of the local authorities. The converse of the argument which applied to Germany was therefore used for Britain, namely, that Britain's poor showing in the second Industrial Revolution was largely due to her failure to develop suitable educational institutions. This was a widely held view and was an overriding factor that was advanced by contemporary observers and industrialists. However, this is not clearly established and is an issue still in dispute. Other factors advanced were high labour costs, tariff barriers, obsolescent plant and equipment, patent laws and trade union restrictions. Economic historians have since advocated many other causes, such as a failure to develop a machine-tool industry, for Britain's loss of industrial eminence.

There were many reasons why the advance of technical education in particular was held back in England. The first of these was the State's disinclination to intervene in educational matters. Arnold saw this as a main bulwark to progress. 'Our notion of the State', he declared, 'is that of an alien intrusive power in the community, not summing up and representing the action of individuals, but thwarting it'.[4] Robert Lowe, the instigator of 'payment-by-results', stated: 'I hold it as our duty not to spend public money to do that which people can do for themselves.'[5] There was a genuine and widespread fear that State intervention would lead to State control. Herbert Spencer in *State Education—Self Defeating* wrote: 'On the whole the experience of the past is proof of the danger of government interference, and of the instability of extreme centralisation, while it affords conclusive evidence of the superior and enduring value of voluntary efforts.' Arnold, however, on his visit to Germany in 1868, found that State control had not in fact materialised. 'Despite State administration of schools there is no political pressure or bias.'[6]

The second factor was the English attitude to education. The concept of 'liberal education' lay at the very root of English educational philosophy. Oxford, Cambridge and the public schools were dominated by the concept of liberal education, an education designed to develop character as well as mind. This was firmly based on the study of classics and mathematics and it was very difficult for newer scientific disciplines to become established. Among the German higher educational circles the dominating ideal was that of 'wissenschaft'—the critical, objective and empirical approach to all knowledge. Thus a constructive attitude towards science was implicit in the general philosophy of German higher education. The emphasis on general education and the empirical approach to knowledge created the right conditions for scientific advance. This factor of liberal education was a crucial difference between the approaches of Germany and Britain. 'The term "liberal education" has acquired a peculiar significance in the history of English culture and thought. Whereas science is the product of French thought and Wissenschaft of German. . . . In discussions on the work of high schools and universities the Germans always talk of Wissenschaft whereas the English talk of "liberal education".'[7]

A third factor was the class attitude to education. Each form or system of education was generally felt to be appropriate to a particular class or sector of society. Thus the terms of reference of the Newcastle Commission, which examined elementary education in 1861, specifically referred to the labouring classes. State provision of elementary schools was indeed intended to be for the industrial and working classes, the middle classes being catered for by a host of private schools scattered throughout the country. The terms of reference of the Schools Inquiry Commission which reported on the endowed grammar schools in 1868 made it clear that the schools included in the inquiry were those intended for the middle classes. Until late in the nineteenth century the universities were the preserve of the middle and upper classes and their studies in any case were rather limited. Technical education was considered to be a lower, rather than a different, form of education; it was held to be appropriate for artisans but not for the middle classes.

Following Lyon Playfair's warning after the 1851 Exhibition, that in the future industrial success would go to the educated nation, increasing attention was given to education, and the new emphasis was a consequence of the fear of being left behind in the race for industrial supremacy. In this new thinking the interdependence of education and industry, and the economic implications of educational policies, loomed large. Unfortunately, at an early stage it was decided that what Britain lacked was an efficient system for the industrial masses and a science-based training for artisans. Thus, great emphasis was placed on evening instruction in technical schools and institutes of one form or another. As a consequence the secondary schools, and the education of the middle classes tended to be neglected.

Like all other educational fields in the nineteenth century the origins of secondary education were to be found in private initiative and benevolence. Progress was more stultified here than in any other field of education in consequence of the overwhelming reluctance of the State to interfere. While the State took a hand in primary education as early as 1833, and in technical education in 1853, it did not create a state system of secondary schools until 1902. As we have seen, there was universal recognition that the endowed grammar schools were intended to cater for the needs of the middle classes, the public schools being the preserve of the upper classes. Little thought was given to the idea of secondary schools for the artisan and working class, such an education being assumed to be totally unsuitable to their needs.

The usual procedure for a public-school boy, and for many grammar-school boys, was to go on to Oxford or Cambridge, but the studies in the ancient universities were largely dominated by

10

the classics and theology. In 1867 a sub-committee of the British Association for the Advancement of Science prepared a report on the best means of promoting scientific education in schools. It presented its findings to the Schools Inquiry Commission and one of its main conclusions was the following:

> At present public opinion in the Universities does not reckon scientific instruction as on a par with mathematical or classical; hence the progress of the subject seems enclosed in this inevitable circle—the ablest men do not study natural science because no rewards are given for it, and no rewards are given for it because the ablest men do not study it.[8]

But Matthew Arnold, after his visit to the Continent in 1868, had pointed the way to the future in his *Schools and Universities on the Continent*:

> It is not in Oxford and Cambridge that the great work to be done is accomplished. . . . we must take instruction to the students and not hope to bring the students to the instruction. We must get out of our heads all notion of making the mass of students come and reside three years or two years or one year or even one month at Oxford and Cambridge, which neither suit their circumstances nor offer the instruction they want. We must plant faculties in the 8 or 10 principal seats of population and let the students follow lectures there from their own homes, or with whatever arrangements for their living they and their parents choose.[9]

The process had indeed begun with the founding of University College, London, in 1826, followed by that of King's College in 1828. The founders of University College had looked to Scotland and Germany for their inspiration and it was modelled on the newly founded University of Berlin. It was designed to provide higher education for those members of the middle classes unable to gain entry to Oxford or Cambridge and to provide opportunities for the study of subjects not available at the older universities. In 1851 Owens College was established at Manchester, the first of the 'civic colleges' to be set up on the pattern of University College, London. Other colleges were quickly established in the main centres of population. These colleges had much in common, and

11

as well as giving full recognition to the physical sciences they were also eager to introduce a whole new range of technological studies. Thus, Liverpool ventured into electric-power engineering, Nottingham and Sheffield into metallurgy, and Leeds and Birmingham into mining.

But these were 'civic' universities founded on the basis of the generosity and support of the provincial cities. In England it was not the policy of the State to participate in the creation of new universities and when, belatedly, the Government began to give a measure of support, the sums contributed could not compare with the lavish State expenditure in Germany, nor indeed with the money collected by public subscription in England. For instance, in 1881 Liverpool University College was founded as the result of £80,000 donated by the citizens of the city. When Government grants were eventually established in 1889, Liverpool's share was £1,500. Chapter 2 portrays the difficulties encountered by Liverpool as a result of this Government policy and it is not untypical of the experiences of all the 'civic' universities.

During the 1850s there was a growing realisation among a minority that England was in danger of losing her industrial supremacy. Influenced by this group the Government, in 1852, created the Department of Practical Art in order to reform the Schools of Industrial Design; in the following year a Science Division was added. It was the creation of this Government department which enabled central funds to be made available for technical education; this was the means by which a system of technical education was able to develop during the second half of the century. However, the greatest impetus to the success of the Department's work, and to technical education in general, came almost at the end of the Department's existence. In 1888 the Government created local authorities, and in the following year the Technical Instruction Act empowered local authorities to raise a penny rate for the aid of technical education. Most local authorities were reluctant to take advantage of these new powers but were glad to avail themselves of the opportunity of using funds put at their disposal by the central government as a result of the Local Taxation Act of 1890. In that year the Chancellor of the Exchequer put an extra 6d a gallon on spirits, and Parliament, led by A. D. Acland, persuaded the Government to hand over this 'whisky money' to the new local authorities for technical instruction. Soon local authorities were establishing Technical Instruction Committees to advise them on the distribution of these extensive new funds.

The Science Division of the Department of Science and Art began by recognising certain existing 'schools of science or trade' and granting aid to them. These schools consisted of a handful of navigation schools, and some trade schools.

In 1859 the Department altered its tactics and proposed that any school or science classes existing or about to be established and approved by the Department could apply through its managers for a certified teacher in certain branches of science.

The essence of the scheme was that it enabled the formation of local management committees (of no less than five responsible persons) with their own chairmen and secretaries to arrange premises for the conducting of science classes, the teachers of which would be paid by the Department. The cost of providing suitable premises and of the heating, lighting and cleaning of such premises was to be met by a proportion of the fees paid by the student. The committee was also to be responsible for the books and apparatus and for conducting the examinations on the results of which the payments were to be made. It was this scheme which enabled a widespread system of evening classes to be established in Liverpool under the aegis of the Liverpool School of Science and the Liverpool Science and Art Classes Committee, as will be shown in Chapter 3. The onus and initiative rested with the local committees and 'If at any time the funds do not cover the requisite local expenses, it must be inferred that there is no demand and the assistance of the Department will be withdrawn'.[10]

The central philosophy behind this Government scheme was revealed in the minute of 1859 which stated: 'It is hoped that a system of science instruction will grow up among the industrial classes which shall entail the least possible cost and interference on the part of the State'.

Three things stand out in this statement; it was the industrial

13

classes who were in need of technical education; the cost of the scheme to the Government was to be as low as possible; and the Government wanted to be involved as little as possible.

The Department of Science and Art was obliged in the light of its terms of reference to devote attention to the artisan. A system of fees was drawn up by which the artisan was entitled to attend the classes aided by the Department without payment of fees, whereas the middle classes were obliged to pay fees. Payment of fees was common to most forms of education during the nineteenth century and the ideology underlying the Department's insistence on fees was as follows:

> The payment of fees by the students can be looked upon as the only solid and self-sufficient basis on which a self-supporting system can be established and supported. . . . Aid on account of those persons who do nothing for themselves cannot be justified, committees of schools and classes and teachers are strongly urged at once to impose as high a scale of fees as they consider can be raised.[11]

The Department began in a modest way by recognising five subjects in 1859, but they quickly extended recognition to other subjects and by 1864 twenty-three subjects in all qualified for receipt of aid. When the Department eventually became part of the Board of Education in 1899 there were twenty-five subjects listed in the directory.

By the end of the century the Department of Science was spending £200,000 a year on technical education[12] and the number of students receiving instruction in classes by the Department exceeded 170,000. This was quite a remarkable achievement, for the Department had no powers of compulsion. According to Hipwell[13] the epitaph of all other nineteenth-century educational institutions could be applied to it, namely, the 'Department did great work in the face of great odds'. Hipwell is of the following opinion:

> The Department sowed the seeds of science education for the people, it spread the learning to an extent probably totally unanticipated. . . . it provided indirectly almost the entire secondary education for the masses for thirty years. . . . and because of the

14

insistence on laissez faire and self-help the people of the localities were forced to band together and to take action if they wished to benefit from the advantages offered to them by the Department.[14]

No one can deny the undoubted success of the Department's work within the limitations imposed upon it by the Government. But one is compelled to ask whether this was the best or the most efficient manner of creating an effective system of technical education during this period. In essence it amounted to no more than the allocation of an annual sum, on average, of £100,000 to technical education to be distributed according to a clearly defined set of rules. This 'payment-by-results', it was argued, encouraged teachers to come forward, but their earnings were so low as to scarcely justify the method and in order to make the work reasonably rewarding in financial terms teachers had to take classes in numerous centres and assume a peripatetic role. (In 1871, for example, out of 828 teachers, 352 earned under £10, only twenty-six earned more than £100 and one earned over £200. The majority earned less than £40.) Further, as will be seen in Chapter 3, they had to endure poor premises, inadequate equipment and an insufficiently prepared student body.

The emergence of local committees depended for success on local initiative and the enlightenment of a few leading citizens. But unlike the university and grammar school there was little status attached to working in the field of technical education. The system worked to some extent, fortunately, because there were so many citizens in Victorian England imbued with public spirit and self-sacrifice. In view of the difficulties and problems confronting those who, voluntarily, in the absence of State or local authority organisations, assumed a responsibility for the provision of technical education one can only admire their enthusiasm, integrity and self-sacrifice. Surely there were easier ways of earning the plaudits of their fellow men?

The system, such as it was, erected largely on the foundation of aid by the Department of Science and Art, appeared to be successful, the imperfections and weaknesses hidden by the emphasis on the growing student body. What would have been the growth in student numbers had there been a properly organised and maintained system such as existed at elementary level? Not until the injection of 'Whisky Money' in 1890 and the takeover by the local authorities towards the end of the century were the major imperfections corrected. Did this system—based on Government aid without State or local authority control—produce the right numbers or the right quality of technically trained men?

It is clear from the foregoing that the English educational system was not designed to produce large cadres of trained scientists and technologists. It did not appear that industry exerted any very great pressure to produce such a demand. This was in direct contrast to the situation in Germany:

> Manufacturers have long ago realised the value of highly trained men in industry and have created a demand for them. It acts in two ways. Firstly, industry is recognised as a career for men of superior standing and education; the business of manufacturers' expert is well paid and it attracts numbers who would otherwise go into professional or academic life. Secondly, those who do go in for it, instead of gaining all their knowledge at the works, go to a school to acquire a thorough scientific mastery. The thing is demanded and consequently it is supplied. In England this is only beginning because the need has not been felt.[15]

In 1900 the number of scientists and technologists produced by German universities and technical high schools was some five times as great as the number produced by English universities and university colleges. Nevertheless, although England lagged far behind Germany in the production of scientists and technologists, English society had changed out of all recognition during the second half of the century. It became an increasingly professional society in which the trained scientist and technologist replaced the amateur, who was displaced from the centre of the scientific scene to the periphery. In 1880, for instance, the membership of the Institute of Chemistry was 424 and that of the Institution of Mechanical Engineers was 1,178; by 1900 these had increased to 1,566 and 5,583 respectively.

The approach to the training of chemists represents one of the major areas of difference between England and Germany. The first systematic research laboratory was set up by von Liebig at Giessen in 1826. This was a pattern which other German universities followed and which they were enabled to do as a result of State support. They quickly gained an enviable reputation for chemical training and research of the highest order and, as such research training was not available in England, the leading chemists of this country sought to supplement their education by a period of study at a German university. In 1845 the Royal College of Chemistry was established in London and W. H. Hofmann, who was appointed to the Chair of Chemistry, brought the German tradition of research with him. Others who carried the German approach into English universities were A. W. Williamson, who was trained at Giessen and Heidelberg and was appointed to the Chair of Chemistry at University College, London, and Sir Edward Frankland, educated at Marburg and Giessen, who became Professor of Chemistry at Owens College, Manchester. Industrial chemists, too, such as Mond, Siemens and the Muspratt brothers, received their chemical training on the Continent. This gap in chemical training between Germany and England was never closed and at the end of the century the former possessed far more university-trained chemists than did England. In Liverpool facilities for chemical training of a high level were not provided until late in the century and meanwhile the best training available was that provided by two private individuals (see Chapter 4).

Throughout the century, engineering in England did not have the high status enjoyed by the German engineering profession. In Germany, engineers who wished to enter State service had, after some years in practice, to pass a State examination, and some years later another State examination hurdle was presented to them, success in which enabled an individual to obtain the highest rank. The profession was well served by the State-run Royal School of Construction and Royal Industrial Academy, at which engineers received a high-level training. The position in England was very different (see Chapter 5). H. S. Hele-Shaw, who was appointed to the first Chair of Engineering at University College, Liverpool, had received little formalised education, but as a brilliant youngster had gained a Whitworth Scholarship which enabled him to study at the College of the West of England, Bristol. This College did not have the power to confer degrees and so Hele-Shaw became a Professor of Engineering without having gained a degree. But he was by no means alone in this and the next five engineers appointed to the Liverpool Department were non-graduates.

The absence of academic training in engineering was particularly pronounced during the early part of the century and indeed the Census of 1841 did not include engineering as a profession. The low status of engineering is surprising in view of the reputation of such men as Joseph Whitworth and Henry Maudsley and the distinction they earned for British engineering. But in England there was a great belief in the 'practical man'. Because the early leaders of engineering industries were men who gained their knowledge by empirical methods, 'rule-of-thumb' became the slogan and university-trained men were looked at with suspicion. The ancient universities, by and large, did not view engineering studies favourably—the first Chair at Cambridge was not created until 1875 and at Oxford not until 1908.

The same absence of training was to be found in the mining industry. There were few schools of mining and those that did exist led a precarious existence. Thus Warrington Smyth, Professor of Mining and Metallurgy at the Royal School of Mines, admitted to the Devonshire Commissioners (Royal Commission on Scientific Instruction, 1872) that the Bristol Mining School had been forced to close down. The Bristol School was based on the subscriptions of colliery lessees and the Government also paid a grant initially, but the latter was withdrawn and the subscriptions also gradually fell. Smyth averred that our mine managers were inferior in general acquirements to the Germans but our workmen were superior in practical acquaintance (see Chapter 6).

However, Chapter 6 on the Cornish mineworker also reveals that in Cornwall there was a need to set up classes to improve the basic English and arithmetic of the miner. This reflected the unsatisfactory state of elementary education. The classes arranged by the Miners' Association for the mine workers in technical subjects were not as successful as they might have been because of this.

In some centres the classes were being attended by the middle classes rather than the mine workers. This deficiency in the primary education of the worker was a major factor in the lack of success of higher educational institutions throughout the country. Lionel Brough, Inspector of Mines for the South West District, told the Devonshire Commissioners that the lessees of collieries only occasionally had some scientific knowledge and even this had been gained as a result of hard study at home and after work.

If things were bad on the management side of industries they were no better lower down the industrial scale:

> Abroad . . . the English system of apprenticeship does not exist, consequently the one letter of recommendation which proves that a young man is worth a salary in an engineer's office, or in a mechanical workshop, is a diploma from a polytechnic school. Therefore the schools are full. . . . my personal inspection of the colleges taught me to marvel at the combination of theoretical and practical knowledge evinced by the German professors. . . . This is the foreign system. What is ours? . . . Young men at the age of about 18, enter the office of a civil engineer. Usually few questions are asked as to previous training. . . . the ordinary pupil is a sort of nuisance in an office, only tolerated in consideration of the fee which accompanied him. From personal experience, I can declare that most pupils are so ignorant of algebra that they are not only incapable of working out a result for themselves, but actually cannot apply the simple formulae which are given in engineers' pocket books. . . . Their arithmetic is very shaky, and a knowledge of physics, chemistry, geology or the higher maths is wonderfully rare. The men have too often chosen the profession from an idea that it is pleasant, and because it is guarded by no preliminary examination. . . . The ignorance of some pupils, especially in mechanical workshops, must be experienced before it can be believed.
>
> These young men during three years have the run of the office or workshop. . . . No one teaches them anything; but they have the opportunity of seeing how some actual work is done. . . .
>
> The contrast between the two systems is complete. . . . Abroad competitive examinations keep out incompetent men; in Britain they are weeded out by the result of the struggle for existence. Abroad great numbers pass through the same school, making the

same designs, in great variety, under the same Professors. Here, each man sees different work, but of a limited kind.[16]

While the formalised training of scientists and technologists was a much neglected field in England in the nineteenth century, there was, nevertheless, a great deal an individual could do himself to acquire knowledge. This notion of the individual helping himself was very widespread and it became almost a national creed with the Victorians. It is exemplified in Samuel Smiles's writings, in particular in his *Self-Help—with Illustrations of Conduct and Perseverance*. This philosophy was carried to excess in England and the individuals included in Smiles's biographies were men of exceptional talent who were able to rise to the top in spite of the obstacles and hardships they encountered on the way. Such obstacles are seen in the account of the Liverpool School of Science in Chapter 3 and in the training of engineers in Chapter 5. At a time when what the nation needed was efficient institutions and a rallying to T. H. Huxley's clarion call of 'we must organise for victory', Smiles's doctrine was insidious and helped to feed the myth that England's greatness was due to the discipline and character of individuals in improving themselves by individual effort.

Throughout the nineteenth century there was a widespread diffusion of interest in science and technology and from the beginning of the century there existed an insatiable demand for lectures and classes. Science had become fashionable following the scientific revolution of the seventeenth century, and much of this interest was dilettante, but there was also a genuine eagerness and thirst for scientific knowledge. Leading members of the middle classes gathered together and formed societies, such as the Literary and Philosophical Societies, with vague aims for the 'diffusion of arts, literature and sciences', which were to be achieved by organising lectures and establishing museums and libraries. Their catholic approach is reflected in their programmes of lectures, which were an oddly assorted mixture of topics covering the arts, sciences and technologies. Much of this must inevitably have been incomprehensible to many of them and it is little wonder that by mid-century attendances at lectures were falling.

This may seem a severe criticism of them and must be weighed in the balance along with the positive attributes of the 'Lit and Phils': they provided an opportunity for a form of post-school education, particularly in the sciences, for the middle classes when other facilities of this kind were almost totally absent; they had firm educational objectives and the advancement of science was in the forefront of their minds; their lectures offered an eminent audience to workers in the scientific and technical fields; and, furthermore, because these lectures were printed in the form of *Proceedings*, the knowledge was widely disseminated, and hence there was a great truth in one stated objective of the Liverpool Literary and Philosophic Society, namely, that it saw itself as 'a body seeking to foster original inquiry and learned research'. On the other hand, many members of the middle classes, concerned at the absence of facilities among the lower orders and perhaps anxious that social order and the values of the middle classes should be preserved in society, banded together to form societies which, although adumbrating rather all-embracing aims, nevertheless gave greater scope to participation by the working classes, and in which technical education had some part to play, particularly after the Technical Instruction Act of 1889 and the Local Taxation Act of 1890. Such was the Royal Polytechnic Society of Cornwall, which aimed to 'promote industrious habits among the working classes and to elicit the inventive powers of the community at large', and which became a centre for classes subsidised by the Department of Science and Art. Lastly, the part played by amateur societies—though minor—in the dissemination of scientific knowledge and in fostering an interest in scientific and technical pursuits must not be overlooked. Although, as has been said earlier, the amateur was increasingly displaced by the professional in nineteenth-century England, amateur societies continued to abound throughout the country and Chapter 9 is an illustration of just one of these.

The following chapters illustrate both the shortcomings and strengths of English scientific and technical society in the nineteenth century. Other obvious areas of strength were of course the formation of the Mechanics' Institutes and the creation and development of professional societies, but these have been well documented elsewhere. The chapters here cover three different aspects of the problem of scientific manpower, education, training, and self-help.

PART I
EDUCATION

1   Science in the Secondary Schools

Introduction
No field of education was without major defects during the nineteenth century but none was quite so badly neglected and unco-ordinated as secondary education. Like all other education fields at that time secondary education had its origins in private initiative and benevolence. Progress was more stultified here than anywhere else, in consequence of the overwhelming reluctance of the State to interfere. It was not until the end of the century that the State began to take constructive steps to remedy this neglect.

Britain's wealth, which predated her imperial greatness, was the outcome initially of the first Industrial Revolution, and to the extent that this can be given any dates it covers the period 1770–1840. This wealth was firmly based on the export of cotton and wool and this was so to a great extent even as late as 1914. No country could hope to emulate England's success in this field, but her industrial competitors triumphed in spite of this because of their success in the newer industries of the second Industrial Revolution—steel, electrical transmission and distribution, electroplating, synthetic dyestuffs, fertilisers and explosives, optics and glass. These were science-based industries, and successful production, as well as owing something to organisation and administration, patent laws, cheap labour, tariff barriers and so on, was also a measure of technically skilled management backed up by scientific research laboratories.

This is where Germany in particular reaped the rewards of investment in scientific education and research. It was the German Gymnasia and Real Gymnasia which gave to their management, scientists, and skilled technicians the fundamental education on which later scientific and technical skills could be grafted in the universities and *technishe hochschulen*. Throughout the nineteenth century there was a demand for 'people's secondary schools' in England which would do for the English middle classes and upper

25

working classes what Germany's secondary schools were doing for her population. Such schools did not exist in England until the emergence of the municipal secondary schools and the reform of the ancient endowed grammar schools at the end of the nineteenth century. The purpose of this essay is to examine the evidence presented by Parliamentary commissions on the contribution of public schools and endowed secondary schools to the training of England's scientific manpower in the late nineteenth century.

The Secondary Schools

In the mid-nineteenth century only nine schools were considered to be 'public schools'. These were the nine 'leading schools' of the country reported on by the Royal Commission under the chairmanship of the Earl of Clarendon to inquire into 'The Revenues and Management of certain Colleges and Schools and the Studies pursued and Instruction Given Therein'. The schools were Eton, Winchester, Westminster, Harrow, Rugby, Shrewsbury, Charterhouse, Merchant Taylors and St Paul's. Most of the remainder were at the time grammar schools set up by charitable endowments, which were frequently intended for the poorer sections of the community. The term 'Public School' was beginning to come into use at the start of the century. Sydney Smith was the first to attempt a definition. In the *Edinburgh Review* of 1810 he wrote: 'By a public school we mean an endowed place of education of old standing, to which the sons of gentlemen resort in considerable numbers and where they reside from 8 or 9 to 18. . . . The characteristic features of these schools are their antiquity, the numbers, and the ages of the young people who are educated there.'[1] But there was considerable doubt as to which schools actually belonged. Samuel Butler, who had raised Shrewsbury from near extinction, was annoyed with Lord Brougham for his refusal to consider Shrewsbury as a public school.

The third quarter of the nineteenth century was a long overdue period of self-examination and reappraisal of the English educational system. The Newcastle Commission had examined the education of the labouring classes and the Clarendon Commission that of the privileged sections of society. The Commission set up in

1864 under the chairmanship of Baron Taunton had the task of examining schools not previously surveyed by other commissions. These remaining schools fell into three categories:

1. Endowed Schools. These were maintained wholly or partly by means of permanent charitable endowments.
2. Private Schools. Largely the property of the master who conducted them. It was estimated that there were 10,000 of these.
3. Proprietary Schools. The property of individuals, of companies, or of corporations.

The Commission listed 674 schools, of which 152 ranked as elementary schools. The school population of the remaining schools was about 35,000 or about 70 pupils per school. Of the schools named 163 have since achieved the status of public school and now belong to the Headmasters' Conference. These were the schools intended for the middle classes, but great difficulty was experienced in assessing who these classes were and the educational need they represented. Dr W. Farr of the Registrar General's Office in a memorandum to the Commission pointed out: 'It is difficult to draw the line between what are called the working classes and the middle classes requiring such education as the Commission is inquiring into.' There were 3,072,064 people living in houses of the assessed annual value of £20. 'These persons may, in my opinion, be fairly taken to represent the middle and higher classes'. Alternatively, they could be assessed another way: 'It is considered right and becoming for the higher and middle classes to marry by licence and for the rest of the population to marry after publication of banns. This leads to the figure of 3,060,680.'

The Commission was highly critical of the inadequacy of the supply of schools and of the unevenness of distribution, which was accidental and arbitrary, being dependent on the geographical distribution of endowments. In two out of three towns in England there was no school above the primary level and in the remaining third the school was often insufficient in size and quality. The endowed grammar schools were intended to give at least a higher than rudimentary education and especially to prepare able boys for the universities. The Commission found that only 145 schools were sending boys to Oxford and Cambridge: 'We cannot

27

consider more than 80–90 of all the endowed schools in England as, in the proper sense of the term, university schools, and less than forty of these are sending students every year'. Like the public schools few of the headmasters of the endowed grammar schools considered sending their pupils to London University or to Owens College, the Royal College of Chemistry or the Royal School of Mines.

The Commission also found that by far the majority of endowed schools gave no better education than that of an ordinary national school, and concluded: 'The instruction given in the endowed schools is very far removed from what the country has a right to demand.' One great difficulty was that the endowments were so small and often the neighbourhood so sparsely populated that the schools were inevitably forced to be nothing more than elementary schools. The Commission found many schools to be scandalously neglected. Governors grossly mismanaged their affairs and even misappropriated the endowments. Many masters enjoyed an unshakeable security while doing little work. In several of the schools there were very few boys being taught.

Scientific Studies

The movement to incorporate scientific studies into the public schools received its first official sanction from the recommendations of the Clarendon Commission. The Commission found that even classical teaching was frequently unsatisfactory and that modern subjects were considered inferior and not worthy of attention. It recommended a remodelling of the curriculum along the lines of the German gymnasia; this involved an acceptance of mathematics, modern languages and science as normal subjects.

Among the nine schools examined by the Commission the curriculum was originally confined to the classics, but by 1864 mathematics was taught in all of them—the time devoted to it ranging from 3hr per week in most of them to 10hr a week at Merchant Taylors. The composition of the teaching staffs at the time was 84 classics teachers, 26 mathematics teachers and 18 modern language teachers. Further: 'Mathematics and modern languages share two disadvantages of being subordinate to the principal study which is that of the classical languages. The chief honours and distinctions of the school are classical, their traditions are classical, the headmasters, and where the tutorial system exists the tutors, are men distinguished chiefly as classical scholars, are attached more or less ardently to classical learning'.[2]

The usual procedure for a public school boy was to go on to Oxford or Cambridge. The reason for this was not entirely academic, for, as the Devonshire Commission on Scientific Instruction and the Advancement of Science (1872) pointed out, it became increasingly the fashion among the prosperous classes to add three or four years at Oxford, not for a professional training but rather as a desirable finishing school for social reasons.

The studies in the ancient universities were in turn largely oriented towards classics and a self-perpetuating cycle was created; students who were taught classics in the schools continued their classical education at Oxford or Cambridge and returned to their schools as classical teachers, reinforcing the common values inherent in the public schools and ancient universities. At Repton during the second half of the century, for example, of seventy masters appointed, thirty-five were from Cambridge and thirty-four were from Oxford. No fewer than sixty-three were appointed in classics, there being no appointments in science. At Dulwich College sixty-seven appointments included fifty-one Oxford and Cambridge men, of whom twenty-one were for classics and eleven for mathematics; most of the remainder taught music, writing and languages. Of the sixty-seven, two only were in science, the first being a Jena PhD appointed in 1871. Of sixty-three appointments at Uppingham between 1870 and 1914, fifty-nine were also Oxford and Cambridge men appointed to teach classics and mathematics. The Devonshire Commission considered that the ancient universities were a stumbling block to the introduction of scientific studies into the public schools:

> Nothing, however, can have much effect on the grammar schools and middle class schools of the country, generally, until the universities which give the key to education in the country, allocate a fair proportion of their endowments to the reward of scientific studies. Till such knowledge 'pays' at the universities, the middle

class schools which look more or less to them, cannot be expected to change their course of instruction.[3]

The Chairman of the Endowed Schools Commission (Taunton), set up in 1869, wrote to the Vice-Chancellors of Oxford and Cambridge:

The course of study insisted on by the universities governs the course adopted in schools, and hence the study of Greek and Latin becomes the highest aim of all great schools. . . . As long as Greek is made a sine qua non at the universities those schools of the new type which it is proposed to establish will labour under the serious disadvantage of being cut off from direct connections with the universities through a want of agreement in their course of studies with University requirements.[4]

The attitudes of the ancient universities towards their studies is reflected in the Fellowships awarded at Oxford and Cambridge shown below.

TABLE 1. *Fellowships at Oxford and Cambridge 1870*

	Classics	Maths	Law and modern history	Natural science
Oxford	145	28	25	4
Cambridge	67	102	2	3

The Clarendon Commission found that with regard to the nine leading schools the average of classical knowledge among the young men leaving was low and that public schools were especially defective in arithmetic and mathematics. As to science the Commission were of the view that:

Natural science with slight exceptions is practically excluded from the education of the higher classes in England . . . whereas natural science is taught in all the Grammar Schools. . . we are convinced that the introduction of the elements of natural science into the regular courses of study is desirable, and we see no reason to doubt that it is practicable . . . we say the elements because the teaching must necessarily be elementary . . . we do not desire, nor indeed do the distinguished men who have urged upon us the claims of their

30

special studies propose, that natural science should occupy a large space in general education . . . class teaching for an hour or two in the week will be found to produce substantial fruits.[5]

Opinion among the headmasters was that classics was the best training for first-class minds. Modern studies was for 'boobies' and did not have high educational value. Thring saw some use in science and languages—'there the most backward in classical knowledge can take refuge. There they can find something to interest them'. Frederick Temple, Head of Rugby, was of the opinion that 'The real defect of mathematics and physical science is that they have not any tendency to humanize. Such studies do not make a man more human but simply more intelligent.'[6]

In their scheme for natural science the Commissioners proposed that physics should take precedence over chemistry. This attitude prevailed in all formalised institutions of secondary education in England. The pre-eminence given to classics, mathematics and, later, physics at the ancient universities and secondary schools reflects the undue respect in which Greek 'scholarship' was held. In Germany on the other hand chemistry was held in at least as great favour as physics.

The Commissioners recommended 11hr for classics, with history and divinity; 3hr for mathematics; 2hr for French or German; 2hr for natural science; and 2hr for music and drawing. By present-day standards natural science was only allotted a very modest place in the scheme of things. In the years immediately preceding the Commission's investigation, schools other than the nine had been increasingly turning their attention to the integration of modern or practical studies and several had erected side by side with their classical organisation a distinct department for the prosecution of such studies, into which boys were allowed to pass. The Commission, which was not against the idea of 'modern departments', did not consider such an arrangement suitable for the leading nine schools:

The public schools are, and we think they ought to be, essentially classical schools, and we do not think it advisable that they should propose to their scholars the alternative course of study, to each

31

of which equal honours must be paid, the one in which a course of Greek and Latin should hold the principal place, and the other a course in which little account should be made of Latin and from which Greek should be excluded alttogeher.[7]

Turning now to the position of science in the various schools, no physical science was taught at Eton, but lectures on a miscellaneous range of topics were given once a week during the winter terms. At Harrow there were a considerable number of masters 'who are interested in science' but there was no direct instruction given in natural science. However, a master had been appointed for natural science and there was a voluntary examination in some one branch of natural science open to the whole school. At Winchester, too, lectures on miscellaneous topics were given once a week. But the Commissioners did not look for much improvement at that school since the Head (Dr Moberly) had expressed the opinion 'that for a school like Winchester . . . science is worthless'.[8]

Very little could be said of science at Westminster, Charterhouse, St Paul's, Merchant Taylors, or Shrewsbury. One famous product of Shrewsbury was Darwin but it could hardly be claimed that the school played any significant part in setting him on his path to fame:

> Nothing could have been worse for my mind that Dr. Butler's school as it was strictly classical, nothing else being taught, except a little history and geography. The school as a means of education to me was simply a blank. . . . My brother worked hard at Chemistry . . . and I was allowed to aid him as a servant in most of his experiments. . . . The subject interested me greatly . . . I was once publicly rebuked by the Headmaster, Dr. Butler, for this wasting time on such useless subjects.[9]

Of the nine schools, the only one which professed to be in any way seriously interested in science was Rugby, where natural philosophy became a subject of instruction in 1849. Initially lectures in natural philosophy were given by a local physician. In the early 1850s a science master was appointed. At this time there was no laboratory and practical science was taught in the cloakroom on the ground floor of the Town Hall. In 1859 a science school and a small chemistry laboratory were built. And in 1859 also a physical science lecture room and laboratory were built at a cost of £1,000. Even here, however, instruction in science was not compulsory and it was in fact regarded as a substitute for modern languages 'to which parents may have recourse if they think fit'. In theory it was permissible to learn both modern languages and physical science and a few boys did actually take instruction in both but the practice was discouraged on the grounds that it distracted the mind with too many pursuits. Instruction in science entailed a fee of 6s 6d and for a further 5gns any boy could also become a laboratory pupil. This did not involve any extra instruction but conferred the privilege of being able to use the laboratory at all hours. Unfortunately in 1861 there were only eight such pupils and the Commissioners concluded that the results were most discouraging. J. M. Wilson, the science master at Rugby, confessed to the Commission that he was a mathematician with no experience of experimental study and had been appointed as a teacher in mathematics, but Dr Temple supposed he could 'get it up sufficiently for the purpose' and so he grafted physical science on to the mathematics. The only other official teacher of science amongst the nine schools was L. M. Stewart at Charterhouse. His subject was chemistry but like Wilson he was not qualified to teach it, having picked it up in his spare time.

Rugby was the most progressive of the nine schools and had forged ahead by the time the Taunton Commission reported. By that time there were lectures in mathematics, geology and chemistry and there were laboratories for physics and chemistry. Twenty-one boys were going through a complete course of analysis, at the end of which they were tested by a rigorous system of examinations. The other masters at Rugby were all in favour of the results of this scheme, for classical scholarship had not suffered as a result: 'It is believed that no master at Rugby would wish to give up natural science and revert to the old curriculum.'[10]

Turning to schools other than the nine, the Commission set up under Baron Taunton concluded that in the endowed grammar schools 'It is quite recently that science has been introduced and its place at present is an unsettled and unsatisfactory one. In very few schools does it form a part of the regular curriculum, there is often, therefore, a want of proper apparatus and material, and the boys who learn are set to do so at odd times or perhaps once or twice a week.'[11]

There were conflicting opinions as to the value of science among witnesses to the Commission. Many were in favour of science and thought it useful as a training of the mind and as an education, but the majority did not regard it as highly as languages and were of the opinion that it was valueless as a training of the mind. Some saw it as an imparting of knowledge after the mind was trained. The headmasters of the grammar schools were just as imbued with the virtues of the classics as were the heads of public schools. The reply given by the Rev J. D. Howson, headmaster of Liverpool Collegiate School, was characteristic of the attitudes of headmasters at that time; when asked whether he did not think it a waste of time that 100 boys should be learning 'Greek grammar when not one of them would be later able to read a Greek book fluently or with pleasure', he replied that he did not think that the time was wasted and that he doubted whether 'in the present condition of education the time could be better spent'.[12]

Among public school masters opinion was unanimously against science but among the endowed grammar schools there was 'the greatest diversity of opinion as to its value. Some hold the strongest conviction of the importance, others express hesitation and misgiving and doubt if it has a place of any real value as an educational instrument; and a few discredit its utility entirely.'[13]

But the cause of science probably suffered as much from indifferent teaching as from its absolute exclusion from the schools. 'At present it not uncommonly happens that natural science, accepted as a necessity is delegated to some master of no great mark, whose task it is to get up as much information about it as may be supposed sufficient. . . . This master, besides being wanting in all but the most superficial acquaintance with his subject, is often ill-supplied with apparatus, as well as deficient in skill in manipulation. . . . In other cases it is thought that all the demands of natural science may be met by engaging an occasional lecturer to deliver a few popular lectures. . . . We cannot wonder that when it is treated in this way it should be pronounced superficial and incapable of disciplining the mind.'[14]

The endowed grammar schools catered for the needs of the middle classes, among whom there was a demand for professional and 'useful' studies such as did not exist among the gentry and aristocracy. The very idea of useful or 'utilitarian' studies was an anathema to most headmasters and teachers in the public and grammar schools. One leading head wrote that a scientific education would be 'useful' but went on to point out:

> . . . and no sooner have I uttered the word useful than I imagine the hideous noise which will environ me and amid the hubbub I faintly distinguish the words vulgar, utilitarian, mechanical. . . . Well, before this storm of customary and traditional clamour I bow my head, and when it is over, I meekly repeat that it would be more useful. . . . One would really think that it was a crime to aim at the material happiness of the human race . . . two or three truths ought now . . . to be regarded as axiomatic. First, that science is as important a means of training as literature; secondly, that every education is one sided and most imperfect which does not add science to literature, thirdly, that our present system is neither literary nor scientific; and fourthly, that it is perfectly possible for it to be both.[15]

James Bryce, Commissioner for the North West, concluded that the subject was taught in three ways. Firstly, in a few schools, for example Liverpool Institute High School, chemistry had been selected as the most suitable and protracted study and the training was thorough and intelligent. Secondly, in a few schools—not more than ten in all—a regular but limited study of a subject was carried on; physics or chemistry was taught in a select class once or twice a week. Lastly, in many expensive schools lectures were given from time to time.

The Devonshire Commission's terms of reference were broader than those of either the Clarendon or Taunton Commissions. Criticisms of the public schools and endowed grammar schools made by the Clarendon and Taunton Commissions were further reinforced by the Devonshire Commission. The Commission listed three kinds of school. Eton, Rugby and Westminster were of the same type, in which there was only one main line and that classical. Other main line schools offered an option of subjects and boys could study science if they desired. These included the City of London, Dulwich, University College School and Taunton. Schools with a modern side by this time included Wellington College, Rossall School, Harrow, Winchester, King's College School, Clifton College, Marlborough College, Cheltenham College for Boys and Christ's Hospital. The Devonshire Commission sent out 205 circulars to the schools enquiring as to what effect science teaching had had. In their replies only two of the schools were able to claim successes on the part of their past pupils. The City of London School submitted a long list of successes and in 1864 four pupils of that school had gone to the University of London to study science and nine to the Royal School of Mines. University College School mentioned thirty-four honours degrees in natural science at Cambridge and forty at London.

Two hundred and five circulars were sent out of which one hundred and twenty-eight were returned. The results are listed in Table 2 below.

TABLE 2 *Science in Secondary Schools*

RETURNS 128

No of schools in which science is taught	63
No having a laboratory	13
No having limited apparatus	18
No of boys in the schools	8,945
No learning science	2,430

The time devoted to science ranged from 4 to 8hr a week at Manchester and Dulwich Grammar Schools to 1hr at the City of London. The schools absolved themselves by claiming that there was an absence of funds, that the educational value of science had a low rating at the universities and that there was difficulty in finding time for this new study in an already over-crowded curriculum:

We regret to observe in many of the larger schools the number of science masters is totally inadequate. We fear that the fewness of the science masters in the great schools and the slowness with which their number is allowed to increase, must, to a certain extent, be due to an inadequate appreciation, on the part of the authorities of those institutions of the importance of the place which science ought to occupy in school education.[16]

The Commissioners of 1868 had made a special study of a 'few schools of unusual magnitude and importance'. One of these was King Edward VI's School, Birmingham. Referring to the school the Commission said:

> The difficulty is, on a large scale, that which occurs in so many of the old endowed schools in the country; that a large machinery for high classical education is provided for a population only a few of whom really want to avail themselves of it, the school is divided into two departments—the English and the Classical. . . . In the Classical department the course of education is determined exclusively with a reference to the old universities; yet not more than four boys a year go from it to those universities. From the fifth class downwards is to be found a mass of boys who clearly, according to the fitness of things, ought not to be in the Classical Department at all. . . . On the whole the Classical Department has set itself to teach Classics with a supplement of maths and little else; while yet many boys leave that department for business at 16 and they will have learnt scarcely anything but the elements of Latin and Greek.[17]

At Tonbridge the Commission found that there had been physical science classes but those had been discontinued. Very little encouragement was given to mathematics and other studies. There was no mention of science at Monmouth, or Christ's Hospital, while at St Olave's (Southwark) there were occasional lectures and at Bedford it was taught from books.

James Bryce was of the opinion that the two Liverpool schools, Liverpool Institute High School and Liverpool Collegiate, were among 'the outstanding day schools of England'. Both were more progressive in their attitude to science than other schools in the country, but the Institute seems to have been the more advanced of the two. The Rev J. Jones, the Headmaster, in evidence to the Taunton Commission, stated that chemistry was flourishing in the school.[18]

Cheltenham College had a modern or military and civil department in which experimental science was taught. Rossall School, founded to give an education to the sons of clergymen, as well as providing a classical education similar to the public schools, had a modern side in which no Greek was taught. A revolutionary departure was that it had five classes—military, naval, civil service, civil engineering class and mercantile class.

The overall position in the public schools of England around the 1870s was that science was taught in fewer than 20 per cent of the schools and to fewer than 10 per cent of the pupils.

The Public School Product

While acknowledging that there were serious defects in these schools, the Clarendon Commissioners were firmly of the opinion that England was very much in the debt of the nine schools:

> Among the services which they have rendered is undoubtedly to be reckoned the maintenance of classical literature as the staple of English education, a service which far outweighs the error of having clung to these studies too exclusively. . . . It is not easy to estimate the degree in which the English people are indebted to these schools for the qualities in which they pique themselves most . . . for their capacity to govern others and control themselves, their aptitude for combining freedom with order, their public spirit, their vigour and manliness of character, their strong but not slavish respect for public opinion, their love of healthy sports and exercises . . . and they have had perhaps the largest share in moulding the character of the English gentleman.[19]

This statement reflects the essential ideology underlying the public school system and such overwhelming testimony in favour of the public schools was not altogether surprising in view of the composition of the Commission. The Taunton Commission in its recommendations stated that due regard should be paid to the spirit of the founders' wills, whose intention was to provide education and to give openings to poor boys of exceptional ability. The founders wished to produce 'cultivated' men by providing a 'liberal education'. However, the course of instruction 'is too narrow. . . . The country is, in some places, thickly dotted with

38

grammar schools, which have fallen into decay because they give undue prominence to what no parents within their reach desire their children to learn.'[20]

In the early and middle part of the century the Victorian middle classes pushed through many schemes of qualifying and competitive examination for entry to the professional bodies. Despite this they remained 'wedded' to the outmoded liberal education of the public schools and increasingly accepted it and its values.

W. J. Reader explains this in terms of the professional man's over-riding concern with social standing and his desire to get as near as possible to the pattern set by the landed gentry. The new-found prestige and enhanced status of the public schools after mid-century were an irresistible attraction and, added to this, entry to Oxford or Cambridge at that time was largely gained through the public school.

The nature of professional society changed radically during the last quarter of the century. The clergy declined in numbers and the medical profession increased, but the most significant change of all was the emergence of engineers and scientists as professional classes. This phenomenon is further reflected by the creation of professional societies to accommodate the needs of this new class. For example, the Iron and Steel Institute was established in 1869, the Physical Society in 1874, the Institute of Chemistry in 1877, the Institute of Mining Engineers in 1889, and the Institute of Mining and Metallurgy in 1892.

The Commission set up under the Chairmanship of Sir J. J. Thompson in 1916 to review the position of natural science in England's secondary schools commented on the loneliness and dejectedness that the few pioneers of scientific studies in the public and grammar schools of the nineteenth century must have felt in the face of their colleagues and headmasters who were openly hostile and who regarded scientific studies as educationally worthless.

While the struggle was going on in the public and grammar schools, scientific studies were advancing in Mechanics' Institutions, technical institutes and in the new civic universities. Many of the former were to become Municipal Secondary Schools and science became a recognised and respectable study in these schools before it was universally acknowledged as academically respectable in the traditional schools. For the greater part of the nineteenth century the products of traditional schools made an insignificant contribution to the scientific and technological élite of the nation, as can be seen from the Appendix at the end of this chapter.

The State, too, had neglected the support of science. This is borne out by the comments of some of the witnesses to the Royal Commission on Scientific Instruction in the 1870s:

> It is acknowledged that Science is neither recognised, nor paid nor rewarded, by the State as it ought to be, that mainly owing to this, there is no career for Science and that parents and masters are justified in avoiding it.

> I believe that natural science has been cultivated in England and maintained at a high level, in a great measure, by the exertion of the scientific societies. The Government has hitherto done hardly anything, and yet science has produced in England great results throughout its natural growth and chiefly in connection with societies.

> The State does not at present by any of its acts, acknowledge pure science as an element of national greatness and usefulness and progress.[21]

In indicting the State these witnesses of the contemporary scene were also indirectly indicting the public schools, for those in positions of power and authority were themselves products of the public schools. It required a great and sustained campaign spread over the greater part of the century by the 'new men' of the 'scientific lobby' to change the schools and educational ethos of the country and to bring about a realisation of the interdependence of science and national greatness.

The Thompson Commission, referred to earlier, pointed out that the neglect of secondary education as a whole, and of science in particular, had disastrous repercussions on the training of technical and scientific manpower in England, for it had led to a shortage of highly qualified specialists in industrial research at the outbreak of World War I.

APPENDIX

*The Public School Product in the Nineteenth Century**

	Numbers	Per cent
No of pupils in survey	3,076	
No going on to Oxford	583	19
No going on to Cambridge	517	17
No entering the army	628	20
No entering law	289	9
No entering the Church	517	17
No entering medicine	80	3
No studying classics	88	8
No studying mathematics	20	6
No studying science	39	1
No studying engineering	125	4

* Being a survey of former pupils of Eton, Harrow, Rugby, Marlborough, Millhill and Dulwich College.

From: *The Vocational Aspect of Education* (Summer 1971) Volume XXIII, no 55

2 Scientific Studies in the University of Liverpool

Liverpool University was a typical product of the municipal enterprise of the second half of the nineteenth century—national policy being such that it contributed in no way to the University's existence. Throughout this period national policy towards education was influenced to a considerable degree by Sir Lyon Playfair's seminal remarks following the Great Exhibition of 1851, and while most of the country was content to bask in the euphoria created by national success at this event Playfair took pains to point out that 'As surely as darkness follows the setting of the sun, so surely will England recede as a manufacturing nation, unless her industrial population becomes more conversant with science than they are now.'[1]

This warning was taken up and reiterated again and again by others throughout the second half of the century. It led to renewed emphasis being put on the education of the 'artisan' and to the creation of the Department of Science and Art for the support of such education. It was argued that what was needed to put England right industrially was an improvement in the general education and the training of artisans.

In 1870 there existed four universities in England, namely, Oxford, Cambridge, London and Durham. Despite the reforms of the 1850s, when Oxford established the Honour School of Natural Science and Cambridge the Natural Science Tripos, these universities had little to offer in the sciences. For many years the number of students entering for these courses was pitiably small and most fellowships and entrance scholarships were in classics. For a Liverpool student the alternative to residence at one of the four universities (or a Scottish university) was a period of continuous instruction at an institution 'recognised' by London University for conferment of its degrees. Manchester had such an institution in the shape of Owens College and the absence of a similar establishment at Liverpool was keenly felt.

In 1857 the Directors of the Mechanics' Institution in Liverpool set up a separate department specifically for this purpose, namely, Queen's College. This was never a success and in 1881 it was finally disbanded; during its twenty-three years of existence only nine students had taken the matriculation or graduate examinations of London University. Other tentative efforts were made to establish a Higher College of Education. One venture involved the transformation of the Royal Institution (founded in 1814 for 'promoting the increase and diffusion of Literature, Art and Sciences') and the other the School of Science (established 1861—now part of the Polytechnic) but nothing came of these attempts. The turning-point in the establishment of a Higher College in Liverpool came when a Town Meeting was held on 24 May 1878. A committee was set up and it was resolved:

That it is desirable that a College be established in Liverpool to provide such instruction in all branches of a liberal education as will enable residents in the town and neighbourhood to qualify for degrees in Science and Arts and at the same time to give such technical instruction in physics, engineering, navigation, chemistry and allied subjects as would be of immediate service in professional and commercial life.

The emergence of the 'civic' universities such as Liverpool was the consequence of strongly felt local and national needs. On a local level they were to provide an alternative liberal education from that of Oxford and Cambridge. At the same time they were to fulfil a national need by creating a supply of highly trained, scientific and technical manpower about which neither the Government nor the ancient seats of learning seemed to be unduly concerned.

In listing its priority for chairs the committee gave precedence to physics, mathematics and engineering, as in its opinion these were the most urgently needed in Liverpool. It appealed to all leading men in the arts, science and literature, and guarantees of £60,000 were immediately obtained for six chairs, three of which were to be in the sciences—chemistry, natural history, and mathematics and experimental physics. When the College began, five appointments to chairs were in fact made, three being the science chairs already named. Shortly afterwards a separate chair of mathematics was created and in 1888 a chair of engineering was added. By the end of the first term the Registrar was able to announce that over 500 students had attended classes at the College but, as in the case of Queen's College, evening classes were the most popular and fewer than 100 students registered for the day classes.

University College, Liverpool, along with all other higher educational institutions in the nineteenth century, suffered from the absence of an efficient system of primary and secondary education. The work initially was of a very low standard, and many students were under sixteen and even fifteen years of age. Owing to the considerable numbers of ill-prepared entrants, classes were provided for matriculation examinations and such classes were the largest in the College. The first graduate examination success was not until 1888 and prior to 1890 there were fewer than a dozen such successes. In 1893 for instance, over 700 names were registered in the College Address Book, nearly 150 of them studying science or engineering, but there were only three BSc honours degrees awarded that year.

Meanwhile, in 1884, the University College had become a constituent college of the Federal University of Victoria. Standards were quickly raised and the rate of expansion was such that by 1900 it was considered that the College now qualified to rank as an independent university. A petition for a University Charter was successful in 1903 when University College became the University of Liverpool.

At Liverpool in 1910 only 24 per cent of the science posts were in mathematics and physics, whereas by contrast 45 per cent of the science posts at Cambridge were in these subjects, but the range of courses provided at Liverpool, particularly in chemistry and engineering, was greater and courses were available in naval architecture, biochemistry, agriculture, sea fisheries and marine biology. It is surprising that a chair of geology was not created until World War I, and for many years geology was taught only in evening classes, by a Mr Lomas, who was not a member of the University staff. Despite the fact that there was no chair in physical chemistry until 1903, this subject had been taught since the 1880s, as it was an essential subject for the Victoria University BSc honours in chemistry. Organic chemistry, too, had been taught from the commencement of the College, and another compulsory subject was technological chemistry, which involved the study of gas analysis and of alkali and allied manufactures. Another obligatory paper in the Victoria BSc honours chemistry was the 'History of Chemistry and the Development of Modern Chemical Philosophy' and by 1914 there was a chair at Liverpool in the Philosophy and History of Mathematics. These developments are of significance in view of the re-awakening interest at British universities in the history of science as an academic subject. Liverpool, too, was among the first universities to include bio-chemistry in its studies and in 1902 a chair was created in that subject.

Between 1882 and 1914 the number of staff in science and engineering increased from four to sixty. The teaching load in the first two decades was such that the opportunity to pursue research was limited. In any case, research was not considered to be a requisite function of universities in England at that time. For a newly qualified graduate the prospects were poor. As Ramsey Muir, a young lecturer at the College, wrote in 1901:

> If a qualified student comes to University College at present and announces that he is prepared to give his time and energy without payment to the pursuit of some scientific investigation, he has to be told that he must pay all the cost of the work.[2]

It was not until the late 1890s, by which time research scholar-ships had been instituted and departmental staffs had expanded, that research began to play a significant role. By 1907 there were twenty-five science research students and five engineering research students. In that year fifty-five research papers were published and these involved thirty-four names; by 1913 there were 107 papers and sixty-six names. Even so, up to 1914 only ninety-nine research scholarships in all had been awarded. Prior to 1900 the best opportunity to pursue research was by means of an appoint-ment as assistant to a professor, but few such posts were available.

In 1896, for instance, the College science and engineering departments had a complement of six professors, two lecturers and fourteen other staff, but, while wealthy citizens and industrialists were prepared to endow chairs in science and engineering, it was left to the University to find money for the junior posts.

At the time of the agitation for a University of Liverpool one of the leading protagonists in the cause was Ramsay Muir. In his *Plea for a University of Liverpool* in 1901 he pointed out that only Turkey had fewer universities in proportion to the population than England. In England universities were thought of as useless luxuries or graceful ornaments, whereas in other countries they were thought of as objects of practical utility—'as the service and support of national greatness'. Sir Eric Ashby recently translated this into modern terms when he described a university as a national investment—the producer of a desirable consumer commodity, ideas which contrast with Disraeli's conception of the university as a 'place of light, liberty and of learning'.

The total capital value of Liverpool University College in 1901 was £450,000 and the annual income £25,000. This income did not meet the necessary expenditure and a special Sustentation Fund had been set up, consisting of donations from friends of the College. In Muir's view this formed:

> . . . a precarious and undignified means of supporting a great institution. A university should not have to depend upon charitable subscriptions . . . Even with the Sustentation Fund, however, it is found impossible to make both ends meet. On the last financial year there was a deficit of £1,250 and the total accumulated debt amounts to over £11,000.[3]

In Germany the annual income of a university ranged from £50,000 to £150,000, the State's contribution to this being nearly 80 per cent. Of the College's income of £25,000 in 1901 the Government contributed 12 per cent, a further 8 per cent coming from the local authority (see Table 1, p 48). In America it was estimated that £1 million was the minimum capital required to create a university but Muir conservatively asked for half a million to transform University College into a University. Liverpool's merchants could not hope to compete with the scale of American private enterprise or the lavish German State subsidies but their support and generosity helped to create in turn the University College in 1881, the University in 1903, and finally assisted in the progression of the University to the forefront of English universities.

State aid to universities began in 1889 when a Treasury grant of £15,000 was distributed amongst them. Liverpool's share, which was £1,500, was subsequently increased to £3,000 in 1897, to £7,700 in 1904 and to £12,850 in 1905. In all, during the period 1889–1914, exchequer grants to the University amounted to some £170,000—not much greater than the annual grant to some individual German universities. Not until 1905 did the Government grant exceed income from endowments and donations. The annual income was inadequate for financing all the necessary projects and the Sustentation Fund had been created to supplement the income. However, contributors to this Fund were frequently the same persons who endowed chairs, gave donations for buildings and laboratories, maintained the Technical College (formerly the School of Science) and supported the secondary schools prior to their take-over by the City Council. Education in Liverpool owed a great deal to a small number of influential families such as the Derbys, the Rathbones, the Muspratts and the Holts.

Although State intervention had not led to State control in neither England nor Germany it was the fear of State control which was nevertheless partly responsible in England for the resistance to the idea of State intervention. One says 'idea of State intervention', for it can hardly be claimed that governments made any strenuous efforts to overcome the resistance. No such apathy or resistance existed in Germany, and the most striking and characteristic feature which distinguished England and Germany in the nineteenth century was the difference in attitude adopted towards State intervention. Matthew Arnold summed this up:

> There are two chief obstacles which oppose themselves to our consulting foreign experience with profit. One is our notion of the State as an alien, intrusive power in the community, not summing up and representing the action of individuals but thwarting it. . . .
> The other is our high opinion of our own energy and prosperity.

State intervention had helped to create in Germany a cohesive and integrated system of education, and the German schools, technical colleges and universities were the envy of scientists and educational reformers in England. In nineteenth-century Liverpool by contrast there was nothing resembling an 'integrated' system of education and the 'ladder' from the elementary school to the University was virtually non-existent.

TABLE 1. *The Finances of University College, Liverpool and of the University of Liverpool*

	1894–5 %	1900–1 %	1913–14 %	1966–7 %
Annual income from:				
Treasury grants and other government sources	9	12	32	80
Local authorities*	14	8	15	1
Fees	38	52	25	8
Endowments and donations	39	28	24	1
Other sources	—	—	—	10
Total annual income (£):	16,000	25,000	84,000	6 million

* As well as Liverpool and Lancashire other local authorities who contributed were Bootle, Cheshire, Birkenhead, Wigan and St Helens.

From: *History of Education Society Bulletin* (Autumn 1969), no 4

3 Technical Education: the Liverpool School of Science

The Liverpool School of Science began in 1861 when classes were held in the Free Library with the support of the Science and Art Department.[1] At the time of the formation of the School, the Free Library Committee was not allowed to perform the work of evening instruction unless the classes were free. To overcome this an independent committee was constituted which collaborated with the Library and Museum Committee and the Department in the running of the classes. The Free Public Library and Museum had been the generous donation of Sir William Brown to the city in 1857. Together with the Mayor (S. R. Graves) and other gentlemen, Brown came to the conclusion that 'the building would not be complete until it had attached to it a School of Science for the benefit of all classes but especially the artizans. That lectures should be delivered and classes held where students could obtain at a small charge scientific information of the contents of the Museum and also receive technical instruction respecting the various trades in which they were respectively engaged.'[2]

At a meeting in the Town Hall in February it was resolved: 'That it is highly desirable that there should be established in Liverpool an institution, the object of which shall be to aid the industrial classes and others in obtaining instruction in science and that the same should be in connection with the Free Library and Museum.'[3]

At a further meeting in the Town Hall in October, presided over by Earl Granville, Lord President of the Privy Council, and supported by the Rt Hon W. E. Gladstone, Chancellor of the Exchequer, it was resolved: 'That it is highly desirable that the means of obtaining instruction in the leading branches of science should be extended in Liverpool.'[4]

As a result the School of Science was established and the Library Committee undertook to grant the free use of the Lecture Hall and other accommodation.

Early Financial Problems

The School, started with so much idealism and so many high hopes, was to pass through several financial crises before it finally succeeded. Many were the difficulties in the initial years and some of these were to persist into the twentieth century. For a long time the main obstacle to be overcome was financial. Originally £3,000 had been raised by subscription, but the School was soon asking for further support from the Department and from the Corporation. The *Annual Report* of 1875 spoke of 'the great want of proper accommodation and of apparatus' and of a debt of £100. The treasurer in the 1878 *Report* said that work was being carried on at a nominal figure. In 1884 'efforts had been made, in the absence of increased public support to induce the teachers to contribute more towards the cost of maintenance'. The Committee conceded it could not push this line of economy too far for fear of losing teachers. The *Report* of 1878 commented:

> The Committee should here commend to the public notice the examples shown by Sheffield, Nottingham, Leeds, Manchester and other larger towns where the expenses of the evening science classes are met by the sums of £500 guaranteed by a few leading men. This plan was adopted here some years ago in connection with the Cambridge University Extension scheme; an expensive scheme which has since *fulfilled our prediction of complete failure*. If this be repeated for the Liverpool School of Science the Committee would be relieved of some anxiety but it is much more desirable to have a larger number of annual subscribers than to expect (especially in these bad times) our leading citizens who are already severely taxed, to maintain an institution whose chief and national object is to promote the application of science to the various industries.

The Cambridge Extension scheme was an attempt to bring university standard teaching to the public. It was concerned with the liberal education of the adult and this together with its associations with the University gave it a higher status than technical education. In the underlined statement one can glimpse a hint of jealousy on the part of the leaders of the 'artisan movement' towards those who belonged to the movement for more general culture. The report was right to draw attention to the 'leading citizens' being 'severely taxed'. The voluntary public elementary schools, the secondary schools, the University, the School of Science, the Mechanics' Institution, the Royal Institution and the Cambridge University Extension movement were all privately financed. Little wonder that the School of Science fared so badly in competition with so many worthy causes. The large sums later contributed to the University throw into sharp relief the meagre support accorded the School of Science. No doubt snobbery played a little part in this. Even so, one would have expected industry to give better support. It was reported in 1878 that 'if all firms who employ skilled hands would subscribe one guinea it would keep the School free of debt. An appeal of this kind was made 10 years ago but the only firms good enough to respond were Messrs. Fawcett, Preston & Co; Papyanini & Co; J. & J. Evans, shipbuilders; Verdin Bros; Walker, Parker & Co.'[5] In that year Dr William Siemens on Prize Day commented: 'What surprizes me most is the scantiness of the means by which such remarkable results have been accomplished—I suggest to the inhabitants of this great and rich city that they should come forward and contribute amply and generously to the support of the School.'[6]

In the first few years the number of students depended on the novelty of the classes, the largest of which were geology and mineralogy. When this novelty wore off, student numbers fell and continued to fall until 1866. During the 1867–8 session Dr Birkenhead (the sole teacher) died and, had it not been for the timely intervention of a Dr Carter, the School might well have been forced to close.[7] However, by good management the School survived as the following quotation reveals:

> The future career of the School was not encouraging and as time lent distance to the first impulses, the public interest rapidly subsided, especially when each Annual Report brought with it a statement of falling off of students whilst the debt of the school was steadily increasing. It was in 1866, when there were only 28 students with a considerable debt that it was feared that the School would

51

have to close—but after several committee meetings it was decided to make a further effort—and by careful management and securing the hearty co-operation of both teachers and students the School had not looked back though always in debt, and greatly in need of means for further development, in addition to the payment of existing liabilities.[8]

Growth of Evening Classes

The evening classes in 1861 started on a small scale—classes being held in mineralogy (140 students) and animal physiology (45). In the following year, classes commenced in magnetism and electricity (75) and organic chemistry (24). One peculiar feature was that classes in inorganic chemistry were not begun until 1867 by which time the organic chemistry classes had petered out. These were restarted in 1870, ran for a few years and finally dropped out altogether and, according to the *Report* of 1875, 'For want of sufficient accommodation and appliances to make the subject really popular few are at present disposed to undertake this branch—but there are enthusiastic audiences for physics, geology and mineralogy.' Physical chemistry was started in 1880 and by 1885 there were nineteen entered for physical chemistry and 237 for inorganic chemistry. The latter was the largest single entry, accounting for 11 per cent of the total student entry.

The School earned a Department of Science grant on the basis of examination successes at the end of the year. The Department's examinations were elaborate, three standards being offered, namely, honours, advanced and elementary. Out of 1,100 student enrolments in 1885 there were 561 successes:[9] seven at honours, 139 at advanced and 359 at elementary. It is difficult to assess the standard of these examinations in relation to the work going on at the University College and the Secondary Schools but, by present-day standards, honours was about equivalent to sixth-form work, advanced to 'O' levels and elementary to third- or fourth-form grammar-school work. Of 1,005 class entries in 1904, only 155 (1 in 6) were above the elementary standard. As late as 1903 Michael Sadler, Professor of the History and Administration of Education at the Victoria University of Manchester, found that one-third of the mathematics was within reach of a good pupil in Standard VII of the elementary school, that one half could be taught in a branch technical centre (lower standard than the School of Science) and one-fifth was about fifth-form level of a secondary school.

By 1888 classes were offered in thirty-four subjects, composed of the orthodox sciences, mathematics, physics, chemistry, geology, etc, and traditional technical subjects such as metallurgy, steam navigation, building, but also more novel subjects such as nautical astronomy, alkali manufacture, iron and steel manufacture and even the science of business. To cater for this spread of subjects the staff had also expanded to twenty members by 1885. Qualifications included one PhD, three BAs, one AMICE, one FIC and two ex-Whitworth scholars. It must be pointed out that the School was entirely devoted to evening work and in this as well as in other respects it can hardly be compared with a Technical High School such as every city the size of Liverpool possessed on the Continent.

After the first two decades, the Liverpool School of Science started to grow rapidly and by 1907 there were 1,877 registered individuals undertaking 5,183hr of instruction, ie about 3hr per student. Nevertheless, even in 1903 Sadler found that many students did not complete their courses; by November of that year the attendance had fallen to 79 per cent of the members enrolled the previous October and by the following February only a little over half were still attending. Much of this was, of course, due to the inconvenience of evening work. The meetings took place usually between 7 and 9 in the evening and many classes did not start until 8 or even 8.30 pm.

Problems of Accommodation and Equipment
It would seem that the original arrangement of classes in the Free Library and Museum was an unsatisfactory state of affairs and so it proved to be in practice. Very soon classes were being held in eleven centres, making the 'School' into a most unwieldy organisation.[10] In 1870, four classes only were held in the Free Library and eleven at the Royal Institution out of sixty-four held during the week. The difficulties of administration and organisation involved

in this arrangement can well be imagined. As Dr William Siemens said at Prize Day, 1878: 'On the Continent great schools were erected for Science and Art but in England such schools were carried on by slow degrees—this institution should have a central building where the classes could be carried on on a more complete footing.'

Suitable accommodation may have been a great worry to the Committee; an even greater headache to the teachers was the paucity of equipment. *Annual Reports* continually drew attention to this fact. The *Report* of 1888 went as far as to appeal for apparatus in the following terms: 'The Committee would be glad to receive from friends any one of the following articles, either new or second-hand: a quadrant electrometer, a globe, a telescope, a barometer, thermometers, glass tubes, apparatus for electrolysis of water.' One of the teachers in the *Report* of 1885–6 complained bitterly of the lack of apparatus:

Dear Sir,
I beg to report, with reference to the classes in magnetism and electricity and heat, light and sound held at the Royal Institution that we are sadly crippled for the want of a proper supply of apparatus which are included in the Science and Art Departments' list of the least amount with which a class should be provided. I have ventured to make a list of the more important of these with the hope that if the Committee do not see their way to supply them, and under present circumstances this is hardly to be expected, this may come under the notice of some of our wealthier citizens.

I have also a class on several Saturday afternoons at which the students make some of the simpler pieces of apparatus for themselves. We are very much restricted in our operations for the want even of such things as hammers, chisels, files etc.
                        I am,
                                Yours faithfully,
                                        J. E. Lloyd Barnes.

He asked for a balance, a set of weights, a model of the eye, a galvanometer, test tubes, flasks, beakers and bottles. The *Report* of 1881–2 had commented on the entire absence of models, diagrams and apparatus, and every report remarked on the fact that apparatus was becoming obsolete. Not only did the shortage of suitable apparatus make practical work difficult but so did the lack of appropriate accommodation, for it would seem that most of the practical work was performed in lecture rooms. R. A. Sloan complained in 1882: 'I can only repeat what I have frequently stated—that these subjects, being essentially experimental subjects, cannot be taught with efficiency except in an experimental room with appliances suited to the work.' Surprisingly, it would seem that Liverpool was no worse than other towns and cities in England, for the Royal Commission on Technical Instruction reported in 1882: 'Probably in no City in the Kingdom are these classes more flourishing or doing better work than in Liverpool.' The Commission also remarked, however, that 'classrooms are so crowded that many students are obliged to stand'.

The erection of a central building, obviously, would have helped to a considerable degree in overcoming these problems. The Committee complained in 1878:

> Owing to the want of accommodation in William Brown Street the yearly increasing classes have to be conducted in seven separate buildings, within a radius of one mile. If a central building were provided, there is abundant evidence to prove that the town would soon possess a College of Science of no mean character. It is much to be regretted that the Royal Institution buildings in Colquitt Street, which are erected for the promotion of Literature, Science and Art should be to a large extent, rented to trades people etc., instead of being entirely used for class and lecture rooms and the development of higher education.

Again there seems to be a hint of antagonism between the School of Science and the Royal Institution.

Once again the perennial problem of a central building was commented on in the *Report* of 1879–80: 'There is a large house in a central position which would meet all the requirements of the School—but the Corporation were unwilling to let it unless they were assured a rent which would pay a sufficient interest upon the outlay. The total cost of the building is under £3,000. The Committee hope that some friend or friends may be induced to perpetuate their name by securing the building for the School.' The Committee later asked the Corporation for a building at a nominal rent and a small annual grant of £200 but it was declined. Repeated efforts to obtain the free use of board schools and greater accommodation at the Royal Institution also met with no success. A Memorial was presented to the Corporation in 1885 suggesting that the erection of a Technical College by the Corporation would meet with the approval of the people of the city. At the same time it was hoped that if it was not in the power of the Corporation to carry out such a proposal that 'some public spirited benefactor will come forward'.

As soon as a central building was constructed it was the intention of the Committee to arrange for the instruction in technical education to meet the requirements of the technical examinations of the City and Guilds of London Institute. This teaching was, in the event, begun long before the creation of the central building, though such teaching was very limited in its extent. The *Annual Report* of 1885 commented: 'Additional classes of the City and Guilds examinations will be opened as means and accommodation admit from time to time. It is clear that too much attention cannot be given in this direction and the Committee do not view with much jealousy the efforts being put forth by School Boards and Voluntary Schools for elementary scholars.' The technical classes, however, never really constituted a substantial proportion of the work of the School and by 1899 the entries for the technical examinations were still less than 20 per cent of the entries for the Department of Science and Art's examination.

What Liverpool needed was a polytechnic similar to those shortly to emerge in London or a Technical High School organised on the basis of the Continental pattern. The *Daily Post* thought otherwise and set its sights much lower. In a leader (22 December 1886) it remarked:

> It is cheering to be able to state that there are at present 1,500 to 2,000 of the artizan class receiving free instruction in the Liverpool School of Science. Here there is a substantial nucleus of a trade school—the general aim of the trade school would be the carrying forward of the manual training of the working classes after leaving the elementary schools i.e. an evening continuation school to our national elementary school system.

56

In 1885, Sir Philip Magnus, who had just returned from the International Congress on Technical Education at Bordeaux, spoke at the Prize Day. He pointed out that there was unanimity of opinion at the Congress that commercial prosperity depended quite as much on the technical aptitude of the nation's artisans and upon the skill and scientific knowledge of the directors of industry as upon the possession of natural resources. It was not a trade school that the School of Science should become but a top-level technical college aimed at the directors of industry. Magnus went on to say:

> Abroad these classes are supported by societies, chambers of commerce and the municipality. Here they depend in all the towns on private benevolence, supplemented by the aid received by 'payment on results' from the Department and from the City and Guilds of London Institute. Now, it often happened that, although private benevolence is capable of initiating and launching an educational institute the interest flags after a time, some other body calls for public benevolence, and the institution languished. This is the case with many of the provincial classes, which carry on from year to year a hand-to-mouth existence, not knowing where they are to provide the funds to pay their teachers salaries and expenses.

This was a remarkably true account of events in Liverpool.

In 1903 Sadler reported that 'Students are drawn from all sections of the community'. His opinion was in line with the *Report* of 1878-9, which remarked that the School's students 'embrace all classes of the industrial community such as foremen, analysts at chemical works, artificers at local foundries, draughtsmen, joiners, plumbers, gas engineers, lithographers, Board School masters and mistresses, shipwrights, telegraphists, water engineers'. However, an examination of student occupations in 1898-9 reveals that the highest proportion of the students were apprentices of one sort or another, mainly engineers or joiners. In 1875 most of the students were between 17 and 21, though thirty-eight were under 15 and a few were over 60.

During 1883-4 there was a commercial depression and donations fell off. Donations fluctuated from year to year and little dependence could be placed on these as a source of income,[11] as can be seen in Table 1 below. Except for a grant of £300 in 1881 and the free use of accommodation at the Library the City Council did not provide assistance.

When the Local Taxation Act of 1890 provided funds for technical education from the so-called 'whisky money', the task of distributing the new funds was given to a sub-committee of the Library, Museum and Arts Committee, called the Technical Instruction Sub-Committee. Grants were made to a number of agencies in the city concerned with technical education. In the first year (1892) expenditure was £15,335, which was distributed as follows:

	£
The Nautical College[12]	1,535
University College	1,750
Secondary Schools	1,940
The School of Art	250
Science, art and technology classes	2,490
Technical instruction centres	2,100
Evening continuation classes	700
Organised 'science schools'	300
Library and museum, etc	4,270

TABLE 1. *Finances of Liverpool School of Science, 1860–90*

	Annual* subscriptions	Donations	Fees	Government Grant	Total income
	£	£	£	£	£
1862	80	0	—	—	129
1865	84	0	6	—	114
1870	90	10	32	—	172
1875	73	44	97	132†	382
1880	157	119	132	665	1,159‡
1885	142	10s 6d	213	862	1,375
1890	135	15	168	767	1,273§

* Membership fee of 1 guinea.
† Payment-on-results to the teachers through the Department of Science and Art, first awarded in 1874.
‡ School in debt for £74.
§ In debt for £223.

TABLE 2. *Liverpool School of Science: Students*

1861	—	128	1880	—	700
1865	—	28	1885	—	1,092
1870	—	163	1893	—	2,086
1875	—	210	1905	—	1,827

Liverpool Technical Education at the End of the Nineteenth Century
The School of Science was the apex of technical education in
Liverpool. At the base of the pyramid were the evening continuation
schools of which, in 1903, there were fifty-three departments conducted in thirty-three centres. Sandwiched between these and the
School of Science were eleven branch technical centres, which
originated in various ways and eventually came under the aegis of
the Technical Instruction Sub-Committee.

They were devoted, in theory, to higher level work than the
ordinary continuation schools.

The standard attained in the evening continuation schools was
not to be above that of the seventh standard of the elementary
school. There were five faculties in being, but little demand for
mathematics, science and technical subjects, and the work was
mostly in the commercial departments due to the steady demand
for boy clerks.

The evening continuation schools were originally the creation of
the School Board and they were taken over as part of the function
of the Education Committee when the School Board was merged
into that body. In theory there ought to have been a much higher
standard of work carried on in the branch technical centres than
in the evening continuation schools. In practice there was little
difference. Sadler found the work of the branch technical centres
to be elementary: 'Out of 53 classes in maths, science and mechanics
in only 9 can the work be said to go beyond the standard of the
elementary or first stage of the Board of Education. Out of 1,313
entries, not more than 150 are for advanced classes'.[13]

The same criticisms were heard regarding the branch centres and
evening schools as were heard about the School of Science. Much
of the work was elementary, the evening schools in particular being
largely devoted to the recovery of work which had been done once

in the elementary schools. Student 'fall-out' was again high. In 1903 in the evening schools twenty-nine classes were stopped between October and February. At the branch centres the number of students attending on 7 November was only 66 per cent of the number which had enrolled, and by February this had fallen to 47 per cent. As Sadler observed: 'Nothing short of State action can secure the adjustment of hours of employment to the needs of those who ought to be attending continuation Classes'.

The Technical Instruction Committee soon after its inception considered that it had completed the technical educational ladder (outlined on p 61) in the City, but many years later Ramsay Muir was pointing out the deficiencies in respect of lack of scholarships.

TABLE 3. *Evening Continuation Schools, 1903*

	Day scholars	Non-day scholars	Totals
Boys	1,303	3,993	2,861
Girls	754	2,461	1,919

Branch Technical Courses, 1903

	Day school pupils	Others	Totals
Boys	429	1,299	1,728
Girls	327	1,232	1,599

There were 320 teachers at the Evening Continuation Schools earning 5–10s an evening.
There were 56 teachers at the Branch Technical Centres earning 6–13s an evening.

Summary

The Liverpool School of Science succeeded on a shoe-string budget against all the odds. Its scheme of organised scientific and technical classes offered at a reasonable price, and conducted by paid teachers, was of wide appeal to a large section of the public, ie teachers, artisans and others who were desirous of such education.

In its report of 1878 the Committee of the School of Science commented that accommodation was unused at the Royal Institution, an institution devoted to the promotion of 'literature, art and science', whereas their own accommodation was woefully inadequate. It is of significance that the Royal Institution by the end of the nineteenth century was far from flourishing, whereas the Liverpool School of Science grew from strength to strength and exists now as part of the Liverpool Polytechnic.

Organisation of Technical Instruction in the City, 1893

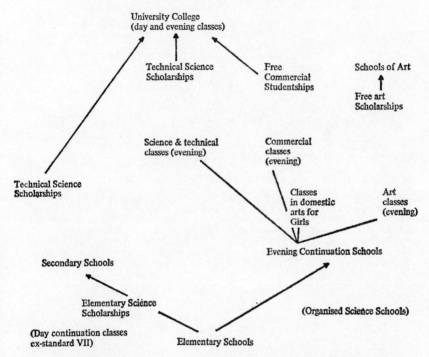

From: *The Vocational Aspect of Education* (Autumn 1970), Volume XXII, no 53

PART II
TRAINING

4   Chemical Training in Nineteenth-century Liverpool

Introduction

In his *Essays on Professional Education*, produced in 1808, R. L. Edgeworth[1] observed that a knowledge of chemistry, which 'every-day promises more and more to be serviceable to agriculture', might be a learned diversion for country gentlemen. Until well into the nineteenth century the value of chemistry was seen to be its 'usefulness' in medicine, drugs and agriculture. The pursuit of chemistry did not lead to any professional status or social acceptance. Its recognition as an academic discipline was also slow to be established. This despite the fact that chemistry was taught at both Oxford and Cambridge in the eighteenth century. It was not, however, one of the more exalted subjects of study at these ancient institutions, whereas the more forward-looking University College and King's College of London University from their foundation in 1826 and 1828 respectively placed the subject on an equal footing with other academic subjects.

During the eighteenth century and early nineteenth century opportunities were available for a certain amount of limited chemical instruction: for instance, there were lectures at the Royal Institutions in London and Liverpool and in the eighteenth century there had been courses at several dissenting academies as well as those given by itinerant lecturers.

Nevertheless prior to the emergence of these two Colleges a more formal chemical training in Britain had either to be undertaken at one of the Scottish Universities or was the outcome of a medical education or an apprenticeship to apothecary or druggist. Such was the case with the celebrated Sir Humphry Davy. In 1826 von Liebig established his chemical research laboratories at the University of Giessen and soon after several other German Universities created chemical research departments of the highest order,

E   65

and thereafter in the nineteenth century many self-respecting British chemists supplemented their British training with a period at one of the foremost German centres.

The Teaching of Chemistry in Nineteenth-century Liverpool
If opportunities for advanced training in chemistry were hard to come by in the country as a whole, in Liverpool they were, to all practical effect, non-existent.

As early as 1822 a Dr T. S. Traill was appointed as Professor of Chemistry at the Royal Institution.[2] From that time until he went to Edinburgh, Traill gave lecture courses in chemistry and he also gave evening lectures and held chemistry classes at the Mechanics' Institution, founded in 1825. The three boys' secondary schools of the City—the Royal Institution, the Liverpool Collegiate Institution and the Liverpool Institute High School—gave due recognition to the teaching of chemistry but perhaps the only one of the three sufficiently well equipped was the Institute High School. This school was highly commended in the Report of the Schools' Inquiry Commission and the Headmaster of the School, the Rev J. Jones, in his evidence to the Commission stated: 'I suppose there is no school in England where chemistry is taught to the same extent as it is with us.'[3]

In Liverpool, as in most other towns in England during the second half of the century, technical education was considerably aided and stimulated by the 'payment by results' awards of the Department of Science and Art. A multifarious collection of institutions emerged in Liverpool following the establishment of the Department's scheme for aiding scientific instruction in this way. Nearly all of these were in receipt of grants under the Department's scheme and many of them included chemistry in their instruction. Foremost among them was the Liverpool School of Science (later the Central Municipal Technical School). Paradoxically, organic chemistry was taught at the School before teaching was begun in inorganic chemistry. The former subject rarely recruited more than twenty students, however, and after some years the subject was dropped. Inorganic chemistry, on the other hand, once begun, went from strength to strength and by 1884 nearly 250 students were being taught inorganic chemistry, and it was the leading subject of instruction.

Another body which organised scientific and technical classes in Liverpool was the Liverpool Science and Art Classes Committee. Like the classes organised by the School of Science, these classes were intended mainly for artisans and were in receipt of aid from the Department of Science and Art. These new classes first appeared in the Department of Science and Art's annual reports in 1871 under the term North District Operatives' Science and Art classes. In the following year similar classes were organised for the South District Operatives and these were held at the National School, Everton Valley, and the Operative Trades Hall, Philadelphia Chambers, Hackins Hey. These classes were immediately successful and quickly sprang up in several centres in the City and by 1875 nearly 200 students were being taught chemistry in such classes. One of the teachers originally engaged in 1871 to teach chemistry was Mr Norman Tate and he later, in addition to carrying a heavy burden of teaching, was appointed Principal of the Liverpool Science and Art Classes. The Committee which supervised these classes was merged in 1892 with the Committee of the School of Science to become the Committee of the Liverpool School of Science, Technology and Art, and this in turn was renamed the Committee of the Central Municipal Technical School at the turn of the century.

Two points need to be made about this so-called 'technical education'. Firstly, all the subjects listed in the Directory of the Department of Science and Art—these included organic and inorganic chemistry, both theoretical and practical—were recognised as falling within the category of 'technical education' as defined in the Technical Instruction Act of 1889, by means of which local authorities were empowered to raise a penny rate in aid of technical instruction. In essence, however, these subjects and teaching constituted scientific instruction and differed considerably from the more industrially oriented technical classes run in connection with the City and Guilds of London Institute. Secondly, it is of interest to assess the academic level of this work. The Department, as we saw in the previous section, conducted examinations at three levels, elementary, advanced and honours, and a reasonable assessment of the respective syllabuses of these courses would be that they paralleled the work done by the middle forms of present-day grammar schools, perhaps at honours level even impinging on sixth-form work. Thus, although the classes aided by the Department came within the purview of technical education, they were in reality concerned with science instruction at the secondary school level.

The first public institution to attempt to teach chemistry at a fairly advanced level was the ill-fated Queen's College—the higher department of the Mechanics' Institution. Queen's College,[4] the object of which was to serve Liverpool in the same way that Owens College served Manchester, began in 1857, and professors were appointed in a number of subjects. It led a precarious existence, however, being a constant drain on the financial resources of the Institute. It was finally disbanded in 1881 and only 260 students had passed through in its twenty-three years. Ironically this was the year of the founding of University College, Liverpool, and one of the four chairs to be instituted at the commencement was in chemistry. The person appointed was J. Campbell Brown, a lecturer in chemistry at the Royal Infirmary Medical School and formerly one of the professors at Queen's College. University College, like Queen's College, suffered from the unpreparedness of its student entrants and, although the chemistry laboratories were among the first buildings to be specifically erected as College buildings, the work for many years was of a low standard; the first honours degree in chemistry was not awarded until 1890, and by 1900 less than thirty honours graduates had been produced by the College.

Against this background of inefficiency and lack of cohesion of the public institutions it is of value to examine what could be achieved by individuals acting alone and receiving no form of aid from the City itself. The following section outlines the achievements of two leading Liverpool chemists who between them probably did more for the training of chemists than all the corporate activity of Liverpool's educational establishments.

The Sheridan Muspratt and Norman Tate Colleges of Science

As this article has shown, the agencies determining scientific education in Liverpool for the greater part of the nineteenth century were disorganised and unco-ordinated. The Government, until the formation of the Department of Science and Art in 1853, showed little interest, and thereafter, despite the mounting evidence and a critical Royal Commission report, were content merely to distribute funds, allowing, indeed insisting, that the initiative come from local bodies and individuals. Two such initiatives on behalf of scientific and technical education have passed almost unnoticed and have not received the attention they deserve.

The first of these was the formation of the College of Chemistry by Dr Sheridan Muspratt. Sheridan, the son of James Muspratt, founder of the 'heavy chemical industry' on Merseyside, was educated at a private school at Bootle and later went to the Andersonian Institution at Glasgow for nine months.[5] From there he went to London and became interested in a small ammonia soda plant being worked in Whitechapel by Hemming & Dyar. He persuaded his father to invest in it and the latter, as a result, lost £8,000. In 1841 Sheridan went to America on behalf of his father, but there again proved a failure—this time selling soda ash and soda crystals. He returned to England in 1842. Meanwhile, James had met von Liebig at the meeting of the British Association for the Advancement of Science at Liverpool in 1837. Von Liebig, the 'father' of organic chemistry, was the creator of the internationally renowned organic chemical laboratories at Giessen University and it was there that James now sent Sheridan to study at the feet of the master. At Giessen von Liebig entrusted Sheridan with the task of elucidating the metallic sulphites, for which he was awarded his PhD degree. Returning from Germany, Sheridan worked under Wilhelm von Hofmann at the Royal College of Chemistry and their work led to the discovery of toluidine.

Sheridan, unlike his father and brothers, proved to be a palpable failure as an industrialist, both from the manufacturing and selling point of view. On the other hand he had considerable research

69

ability and his experience of Liebig's and Hofmann's teaching methods no doubt influenced him in deciding what his role was to be, for he returned to Liverpool and in 1848 opened the Liverpool College of Chemistry in a stable in the back of a house in Canning Street. Probably as the result of the influence of Hofmann, the Prince Consort agreed to act as Patron and so the College earned the title of the Royal College of Chemistry. Sheridan solicited and gained the support of Liebig and Hofmann for his suitability for 'office of Professor'.

The term at the College was two sessions of eighteen weeks each and students brought their own small apparatus, but reagents and gas were supplied. A good library of German and English works was provided and eighteen students were soon at work. The *Chemical News and Journal of Physical Science* in 1870 commented that the course at the College was 'entirely devoted to laboratory work' and the college was open from 10am to 5pm on weekdays and until 1pm on Saturdays. The fees ranged from 8gns per term for two days' attendance every week to 12gns per term for six days' attendance during the week. Medical students were allowed to enter for 1hr per day per session for a fee of 3gns. Certificates of attendance granted by the College were recognised by the University of London and by the Apothecaries Hall of London.

Although the College began in Canning Street, Gore's *Directory* of 1853 lists the College as being in Duke Street and thereafter the address is variously given as 98, 98A, 96 and 96A Duke Street. The last year in which Muspratt's name appeared as Principal was 1871, and in the following year Professor Martin Murphy was stated to be the Principal. In 1878 he was replaced by Thomas H. Johnson, Analytical Consulting Chemist, who, in turn, gave way in 1882 to George Tate, a German-trained PhD, and Granville H. Sharpe. They described themselves as Chemists and Analytical Assayers. By 1884 Sharpe seems to have left, but it was not until 1896 that Tate described himself as the Principal of the Liverpool College of Chemistry, which, by then, had lost the Royal prefix. From 1910 the College of Chemistry is no longer mentioned and in that year Tate is listed as being at the Laboratories, Windsor Buildings, George Street, where he remained until his death in 1934.

From 1880 onwards the College's classes qualified for grant from the Department of Science and Art, and between 1880 and 1896 an average of seventy-five students a year were taught at the College. As far as can be ascertained, no records survive of the work of the College. This is unfortunate, for it would be of interest to know how many leading chemists on Merseyside received their training at the College—for many years the only institution at which such training could be obtained.

By a curious coincidence the name Tate was also associated with the second of these institutions that existed in Liverpool. The creation of this was due to the efforts of Norman Tate—no relation of George Tate. Norman Tate was in fact trained at the Sheridan Muspratt College of Chemistry and he first appears in Gore's *Directory* in 1868 as an Analytical and Consulting Chemist, his address being given as Berwyn Villas, 15 Newstead Road, Windsor South. Norman Tate was born in 1837 in Wells, Somerset. The son of a clergyman, he was educated at the Chapter Grammar School, Wells, and after a few years engaged in pharmacy came to Liverpool. He entered the laboratory of Dr Sheridan Muspratt, where he devoted himself to practical analysis and general chemistry. While there several of his papers were read before the Chemical Society of London and the Royal Society of Dublin.[6] After leaving the Muspratt College he went as chemist to John Hutchinson, alkali manufacturer of Widnes, and was later given charge of the various manufacturing processes and the construction and working of the chemical plant. At the time of the original importation of petroleum from America he devoted special attention to the matter and soon became a leading authority on it.

In 1870 Tate moved to 7 Irwell Chambers, Fazakerly Street, Oldhall Street, where he set up a School of Technical Chemistry. In 1873 he moved once more, this time to 7 and 9 Hackins Hey, where his School became the Liverpool College of Science and Technology. (This must not be confused with the Liverpool School of Science, Technology and Art, mentioned in an earlier section.) Tate, like other analytical and consulting chemists, acted as an independent middleman between merchant and buyer. Chemical firms used palm, ground nut and coconut oils as raw materials for making soap, butter, margarine and cooking fats. The analyst crushed a sample of nut or palm kernels and granted certificates to the supplier indicating the percentage quantity of oil in the samples. Tate's reputation as an analyst stemmed from the West African Trade and his speciality was oils, fats and waxes. The firm of Norman Tate & Co later gained a world monopoly on glycerine analysis for Unilever. According to the *Chemical News and Journal of Physical Science*, students were free to attend Tate's School of Technical Chemistry at Irwell Chambers at any time between 9.30am and 5pm on weekdays and 9.30am and 1pm on Saturdays. His laboratory was open also on two evenings a week for practical work, and lectures were given on one evening of the week. A separate bench was provided for each student and he was also supplied with all ordinary chemicals, gas, and fuel, but had to provide his own test-tubes, beakers and other apparatus.

In 1873 Tate moved his analytical laboratories to Hackins Hey, a narrow Dickensian street near Exchange Station. It seems that these laboratories were also used for the teaching laboratories of his College of Science. Classes were held in a basement hall which still survives today. Gore's *Directory* gives the General Laboratories as 5, 8, 9 and 11 Philadelphia Chambers and the laboratory for the examination of oils and fats as 12A; sample rooms were installed at 3 Ashton Chambers. Classes were held at both Philadelphia Chambers and Ashton Chambers and, as we have seen, these were some of the first operative classes to be run as part of the Liverpool Science and Art Classes which qualified for 'payment by results' from the Department of Science and Art. Between 1880 and 1892 the Department gave grants on behalf of 940 students at Philadelphia Chambers and between 1888 and 1892 for 200 students at Ashton Chambers. Tate received annual payments for these ranging from £18 to £73, but no doubt these were small recompenses for the efforts he put into teaching and training chemists at Hackins Hey and other Science and Art Classes scattered throughout the City.[7] In addition to his great efforts to popularise chemistry Tate taught botany, physiology and general biology three or four evenings a week, and still found time to become Chairman of the Liverpool Branch of the Society of Chemical

Industry and to found the Liverpool Science Students' Association and the Liverpool Science and Art Teachers' Association.

After Norman Tate's death the laboratories were run by two chemists named Windel and Woolcott and in 1892 a young man, Joseph Davies, son of a Welsh father and Austrian mother, came as a junior under Windel and Woolcott. Joseph, born in Liverpool, was educated at St Francis Xavier and probably received his chemical training in evening classes under Norman Tate and Watson Gray, another Liverpool Consulting Chemist. The Liverpool College of Science, Technology and Art asked Joseph to teach the theoretical aspects of the science of bakery and milling, which he did for a number of years. In 1905 Joseph took over the firm and on his death he was succeeded by his son, Edward Leo Davies, who gained an honours BSc degree in chemistry at Liverpool University. The name of the firm was not changed, however, and it still survives nearly a century later as Norman Tate & Co, Consulting Chemists.[8]

As in the case of the Muspratt College, no records survive of the students who passed through the hands of Norman Tate and it is impossible to assess accurately the value and worth of these institutions or the standards of work maintained by them, but it is probably not far from the truth to say that they contributed more to the education and training of chemists in Liverpool than any other institution in the nineteenth century.

It is paradoxical and truly remarkable that in Liverpool of all cities—adjacent to Widnes, the 'home' of the heavy chemical industry—the training of many of its leading chemists should be largely in private hands. In the light of this it is not surprising that many of the firms in the Widnes–St Helens–Warrington chemical complex, such as, for example, Joseph Crosfield of Warrington, were forced to rely to a considerable extent on chemists trained in German universities until virtually the end of the century.

From: *Annals of Science* (March 1971), Volume 27, no 1

5   The Education and Training of Engineers in Nineteenth-century Liverpool

Although by 1914 both America and Germany had surpassed Britain as manufacturing nations, the period up to World War I is notable for the number of people who both forecast this and made suggestions as to how Britain might regain its economic leadership. These personalities were to be found at both the national and local levels, and, although they had less success than might have been hoped for, their influence can be seen in a number of fields, notably that of education.

Nowhere are the problems, and the awareness of them, more apparent than in the engineering field. The first Industrial Revolution had its birth in England, and had been accompanied by many major engineering break-throughs. However, with increasing industrial sophistication such break-throughs and developments relied less and less on the haphazard approaches of the eighteenth and early nineteenth centuries, and more on an increasingly highly trained manpower working in a more formalised research environment. The achievement of such conditions in England was not aided by the low status under which engineers were working, by the frequent lack of training amongst the earlier generation of engineers like Newcomen and Watt, and Trevithick and Stephenson, which supported the myth that an engineer had only to be a 'practical' man, and by a lack of urgency found in the Government regarding foreign competition. Although industrialists and scientists would often voice their apprehensions about the British economy, this was a difficult message for an Oxford-trained classicist serving as a Cabinet member to grasp.

The problems in the field of education and training facing the engineers can be usefully illustrated by the example of Liverpool in the latter part of the nineteenth century and the first part of the

74

twentieth century. Although we use the developments and discussions taking place in Liverpool, it was little different from the
national picture.

A society that catered partly for the interests of engineers was
the Liverpool Polytechnic Society, formed 'For the Encouragement
of Useful Arts and Inventions' in 1838. It was intended to embrace
a wide and varied range of subjects including machinery, mechanical
engineering, ornamenting, chemical science, agricultural implements, the economy of fuel, the application of chemistry and
geology to agriculture, the beauty of buildings, the commercial
interests of the country and the physical conditions of its inhabitants. The objects of the Society as they appeared in the
Report of the Council for 1843 were rather different from those of
other societies. The Council claimed:

> Societies like the present afford the means of friendly union and
> communication between minds of kindred tastes existing in large
> and populous cities; locally and in close proximity with each other,
> but in effect, estranged and distant; separated by repulsive cir-
> cumstances and artificial distinctions, unless a link be supplied,
> which with magnet power shall bring the whole under one common
> influence. It is the design of this society to supply the connecting
> chain, to remove existing barriers and to bring together into one
> centre the inventive talent of this great community.

Such were the lofty aims of the Society and it is to be wondered
how these could possibly be attained. Certainly the papers read
at the meetings of the Society fell far short. These included: 'On
the means of Preserving Documents from Fire', 'On the Improvements of Liverpool', 'The Changes of Density of Metals when
Drawn through a Steel Plate Roller', and 'On the Screw Propeller'.

Papers were read on a diversity of subjects covering architecture,
steam navigation, coal mines, furnaces, railway gauges and so on.
During the 1891 session Professor Hele-Shaw, Professor of Engineering at University College, Liverpool, read a paper on 'The
Transmission of Power by the Friction of Hard Surfaces'. This
embodied some of the results of his researches on friction and he
sent papers on this subject to the British Association, the Royal
Society, and the Institute of Civil Engineers. As well as discussing

75

purely technical subjects the Society also showed concern with social matters. For instance, in 1847 there was a paper on 'The Cruelties of Using Climbing Boys for Chimneys in Defiance of Act of Parliament'.

As time progressed the papers became more clearly engineering in content and less dilettante. In 1888, for example, James Hargreaves gave a paper on his Thermo Dynamic Engine, and other papers included 'Hotkin's Patent Boiler Cleaner', 'Wrought Iron Pipes for Water Mains', 'Improved Steel Sleepers'. From its inception the Society offered prizes ranging from £3 to £10 in order to stimulate and encourage members to give papers, and in 1887 a Mr T. Morris of Warrington won £10 for his papers on 'The Influence of Oxygen on Iron During the Puddling Process and its Effects on the Engineering Shop'.

The first meeting of the Society in 1839 was held at the Medical Institute, Mount Pleasant, but in the following year and thereafter meetings continued to be held at the Royal Institution. Not many years after the Society was formed the membership exceeded 150 but by 1885 it had risen to only 167. It is clear that this group composed a wealth of engineering and industrial talent. As well as the academics such as Professor Hele-Shaw, Dr George Tate and Norman Tate, the members included industrialists such as Andrew Kurtz, Benjamin Platt, Robert Mather and James Hargreaves, and the addresses of the members embraced a large number of foundries and steel works. The Society first produced *Transactions* in 1843 and these were exchanged with the published works of twenty-six other societies. Nearly all the papers read were too technical to be understood by any other than an experienced engineer or scientist and from time to time the Society devoted an evening to an examination of education and training within the profession. On two such occasions papers were read by George Lauder on 'Engineering Education' and William Rickard on 'Technical Education'. They are both worthy of close attention as they no doubt represented the prevailing attitudes of the profession.

The first of these discussions occurred during the session of 1868. Mr Lauder began by claiming: 'Formerly theory was looked upon as something to be avoided—now, however, its true place has been assigned and it is fully recognised.' But he went on to say:

I consider the practical part of an engineering education to be the most important . . . the want of practical experience in the workshop can never be completely overcome. I neither advocate a five nor a seven years apprenticeship, nor the system that seems to be so popular in the polytechnic schools in some parts of the Continent which endeavours to give workshop experience by making it part of the course of study to walk through certain shops and take notes or sketches of machines or processes, nor another system which provides a workshop expressly for the students. The latter may make good toy makers but it is not adapted to engineering science.[1]

Having advanced the very reasonable view that practical education was the most important, Lauder then outlined what to him were the essential things to be learnt in the workshop:

The special education to be gained in the workshop consists of the education of the senses in a special direction. Thus, when a youth has learned to chip without hitting his fingers instead of the head of his chisel . . . again, when he has gained facility in moving heavy masses of material a higher degree of practical knowledge has been gained, a phrenologist would say his organs of weight and size have been activated.[2]

A recent report on technical education had listed University College, London, King's College, London, Glasgow University, and Queen's College, Dublin, as being efficient in the teaching of technical education. Yet in Belgium, Lauder pointed out, there were nine higher institutions devoted to technical education, and in France, Switzerland and Germany many more. Lauder had no doubts as to the cause of this:

We are not blessed with a paternal government which will take the matter in hand and rectify it for us. All the government has done by its capitation grants and such like devices is mere nibbling round the edges and all that it is likely to do, judging from the past, will probably not amount to much more . . . The evil, then must be met by local and individual action if it is to be met at all. . . .

77

Manchester have just raised a sum sufficient to endow a Chair of Engineering in Owen's College.[3] . . . Surely there is sufficient public spirit in our engineers and merchants generally to follow the example set them by Manchester. There is reason . . . to prophecy that our commercial greatness must wane, unless we can provide education for the rising generation. . . . the report already quoted shows how far the mere fact of having better educated people has already advanced the countries which are coming into competition with us.[4]

Lauder continued by drawing attention to a problem later tackled energetically by the Liverpool Council of Education, namely the matter of scholarships from the elementary schools:

On the Continent it is found that in the elementary schools there are scholarships open to the most successful pupils, but hitherto our workmen have been left to do for themselves. . . . Although engaged from 6 a.m. to 6 p.m. at their daily work, they manage to attend evening classes, where these are available, and where they are not, they tread their weary way alone, picking up what scraps of information they can find in the nearest lending library and by dint of their British pluck . . . get sufficient knowledge, not only to fit them for foremen and managers, but in many cases to enable them to take a prominent position in the scientific world in the history of their country.[5]

Lauder himself conducted classes in practical engineering at Queen's College (Liverpool) but these were entirely supported by students' fees, and the College was not endowed. In support of his case Lauder claimed that Sir Joseph Whitworth's bequest of £100,000 to found scholarships was probably motivated by his own experiences during his early days.

The reading of this paper was followed by a lengthy discussion, during which it emerged that opinion was unanimously in favour of more technical education. One speaker dissented from the opinion that as a nation we were losing our industrial position in consequence of the ignorance of our artisans and mechanics. Mr Scott Russell also introduced a dissenting note when he argued that he found the most valuable handicraftsmen were those who could neither read nor write. Dr Hayward remarked that nature

78

made the engineer, but education improved him, so technical education was vitally necessary. One member pointed out that Watt and Stephenson had educated their children and another referred in terms of praise to the German draughtsmen in this country. The Chairman in winding up the discussion remarked that the discussion had been interesting and, although it had been mainly concerned with making a case for technical education and not for showing what was needed, it had not been entirely useless. In conclusion he said that few pupils went to the great schools of this country as compared with Prussia and also that few students matriculated. In his view Britain would not maintain her supremacy and that trade would inevitably go to Germany.

A more useful contribution to this very acute problem was the paper by Dr William Rickard, the Principal of Alverton House Academy, during the thirty-fourth session in 1871. Rickard began by outlining the origins of the circumstances which had led to Britain losing her industrial supremacy:

> For a considerable period in the history of our manufactures, improvements were extremely limited, and more frequently the result of accident than of design, and trial and error appear to have been the only instructors. During this period, however, the possession of vast mineral treasures rendered this country the great workshop of the world, and having almost no competitors, our manufacturers became rich, while the means by which a work was accomplished were often of little consideration provided the work was done, some of our leading engineers being ignorant of principles which are now well-known in every work-shop. . . . The Government looked on complacently . . . and the British workman unaided by the Government has thus far educated himself. . . . The governments of other nations in order to create industries that might compete with us in the production of utilities have been compelled to take the subject into their own hands, and educate the people. . . . It is from these schools (i.e. the Continental schools) that a few spirited individuals from among the most successful students tempted by increased remuneration, have spread themselves into this country and other countries requiring their labour . . .[6]

Rickard cited a conference which had been held to 'consider the most practical measures for improvement in technical education'. A sub-committee had been appointed to 'take such steps as might give effect to the resolutions which were carried at the conference'. The committee concluded that they could not recommend polytechnics for imitation in this country and resolved that 'Technical instruction should not as a rule be given in separate professional institutions but in institutions established for general education.'[7]

In proposing the first resolution at the Conference Dr Lyon Playfair had said: 'The universities are ports into which the ships come from the schools, and the ports must be adapted to the character of the ships they are to receive.'

In Rickard's view, however, the universities should regulate the schools and not the schools the universities. If the universities were to announce that equal honours were to be awarded to science, then science would be cultivated. He referred to the excellent schools of France—the École Polytechnique, the École des Mines, the École Centrale and the École des Ponts et Chaussées. Liverpool seemed to be behind in technical education. Up to May 1868 there was no technical school worthy of the name in Liverpool,[8] but since then 'an improvement had taken place in this respect', ie he referred to Queen's College, which had a faculty of science and engineering. But on the other hand 'I have obtained some particulars of the classes at the Operative Trades Hall, Duke Street, but less than 40 per cent of the whole number entered attend the various classes'.[9] For Liverpool the problem would be solved if Oxford and Cambridge created Fellowships and Scholarships in science for the boys' secondary schools, the Liverpool Collegiate and Liverpool Institute. Alternatively,

Let steps be taken to place the Collegiate upon the same footing as University College and King's College, London. . . . Let its diplomas, whether for classics or engineering be recognised as that of any other University and the great difficulty would vanish. . . . At the Collegiate there are whole buildings already in existence . . . two to three additions to the staff would be all that is immediately necessary. I believe there are at present an excellent Professor of

Chemistry and a Professor of Natural Philosophy . . . it remains to appoint Professors of Natural History, Civil and Mechanical Engineering and of Architecture.[10]

Rickard ended his address by quoting Mr Bernhard Samuelson's comments in a speech given to a Conference of the Society of Science and Art: 'My short Continental tour . . . has convinced me that . . . we have arrived at many conclusions by a system of trial and error at which we might have arrived by more direct means if we had been better instructed.'

Thus Rickard concluded:

This sets before us in a very strong light the course we should adopt to preserve our superiority in those branches in which we are still superior, and to remove our deficiencies in those branches in which we are inferior. EDUCATE! Educate technically those who are intended to perpetuate our skill and our success.[11]

In opening the discussion Norman Tate confessed that in the past results had been obtained by rule-of-thumb method and that workmen, foremen and often the masters were totally ignorant of the simplest scientific principles upon which operations were based. In his opinion a larger and more extended scheme of elementary education was the most effectual method of striking at the root of the evil. As to the poor attendance at the Operative Classes in Duke Street, mentioned in Rickard's paper, the main reason for this was the want of previous education. In a class he himself taught the attendance was regular for three or four meetings, but then it fell off. He asked one of the men the reason and was told 'it was impossible to try to learn chemistry if one had to do with multiplication'.

These men were not able to follow scientific instruction for want of elementary education. . . . The example of Liverpool showed, that what was wanted was elementary education, but this . . . should also include the first principles of science. . . . The pupil might be removed from the elementary school to the workshop, and, by curtailing the hours of manual labour so that time would be afforded to attend trade or technical schools much might be done to further his technical education.[12]

F   81

Present at the meeting was Professor Reynolds, who had been appointed to the Chair of Engineering at Owens College, previously referred to. At this point he joined in the discussion. His own experience led him to believe that before they could learn the applications of science in any shape, they must be acquainted with it to a certain extent in its abstract form. The system of pupilage had afforded very successful results as far as practical instruction went, but it involved a great waste of time and labour unless the scientific instruction had preceded it, owing to the pupil's endeavouring to master a certain operation without understanding the principles upon which it was based. The great requirement for general and extended technical education was, he considered, good primary schools, in order to diffuse more widely the general basis upon which the special or technical part was built. The Government schools under the Science and Art Department already did this in great measure, but the results appeared to him to tend rather to the improvement of a few, thus raised as it were out of their class, than to the elevation of the standard of education among workmen generally.

To Mr G. F. Deacon, who described himself as a lecturer in Civil Engineering and Mechanics at Queen's College,[13] the fundamental question it seemed was 'What is the best manner in which to supersede or supplement the present pupilage system?' He himself, after receiving the ordinary course of education in a classical school, passed into the workshop of a Glasgow engineering firm, where he found himself lamentably deficient in the theoretical knowledge that was requisite. Through the kindness of his principals he was enabled to attend the engineering lectures at Glasgow University, after which he returned to the works with greatly increased interest in his practical work, and with a theoretical knowledge of the subject matter. He held that a system of attending the workshop at one time and the college at another would be an improvement. One thing that had struck him forcibly was the deficiency in mathematical knowledge of engineering pupils in even first-class workshops and offices. On this point Liverpool contrasted unfavourably with Glasgow. The small attendance at engineering classes generally might be set down to two causes: first, the absence of any diploma of engineering science, and second, from that fact that, under the present system, the students could attend only in the evening, when already fatigued with the day's work. He considered that, in most cases, seventeen years of age was quite early enough for youths of this class to leave school in order to commence their technical education.

Another speaker advanced the claim for a good system of general education and called for the appointment of a Minister of Technical Education. This speaker's experience as regards Queen's College also led him to conclude that the cause of any failures lay in the want of good ground work.

Mr Henry Duckworth was the final speaker of the evening and in his view there was no place so behindhand in proportion to its size as Liverpool. His own experience at the School of Science had led him to believe that it was impossible to impart scientific knowledge successfully without a certain advantage being held out to the students. As a rule, almost all who joined the classes were clerks having a taste for science and attended solely for that reason.[14] If, however, masters and heads of offices took a greater interest in science and art and showed that they set some value upon those of their youths who possessed some knowledge of these subjects, then he considered that the science classes would be much better attended. Latterly a movement had been set on foot to endeavour to establish a Science College in Liverpool—he was very much afraid that the proposal would hardly take effect for some time to come. In this, of course, he was quite right, for University College was not established until another decade had passed.

It is significant and apt that of all the Liverpool scientific societies only two showed any concern about such matters as education and training, professional status and the impact of their discipline on the material welfare of the country as a whole, and that these two were the Polytechnic Society and the Engineering Society. It was in engineering and technical education that the country lagged furthest behind the Continent and it was developments in this area that had the strongest interaction with industrial prosperity. For far too long too much attention had been given

83

to mathematics, astronomy and the geological and biological sciences. Probably no country in the world produced so many top-class mathematicians and biologists as did England at the time. Unfortunately the collective productive power of those sciences had marginal effect on the economy.

Secondly, engineers were more acutely aware of professional standards and status because of the low estimation in which civil engineering was held during the nineteenth century.

The same concern with their role in Society and their importance to the economic well-being of the country was shown by the members of the Liverpool Engineering Society, and significantly the first Presidential Address given by Mr Graham Smith was entitled 'The Status and Prospects of Engineers'.[15] The Society was created in November 1875, and its formation 'answered a long-felt need' in the area, but took place unknown to the majority of engineers in the neighbourhood. Under the name of Liverpool Engineering Student's Society it met for 'reading and discussing engineering subjects'. At first it gathered weekly at the Royal Institution, but this proved too much for some of the members, so they met fortnightly instead of weekly and friends were invited to join.

Mr Graham Smith in his Presidential Address claimed that for engineers:

> ... their progress has been gradual, yet ceaseless, and it has been too little attended to by their neighbours. ... We may premise that they are a most respectable class of men ... they have an aristocratic look about them ... an aristocracy tempered by science. ... at the present time the leaders of the engineering profession are totally unrecognised by the British Government. On State occasions the merest subaltern takes precedence over engineers whose energy, ability and perseverance have been instrumental in placing Great Britain on the high pinnacle on which she now rests. Although titles may be showered on corporate dignitaries and the members of other professions, they are sparsely distributed in that of the engineer. ... Notwithstanding the railway mania and the great demand for machinery and engineering work during the past half century, few men have made large fortunes by engineering pure and simple. ... Public bodies seem to form about

the lowest estimate of the value of engineers, possibly owing to the fact that men forming such boards seldom have any knowledge of engineering. . . . Punch's advice to those about to marry. Don't! aptly applies to those purposing to enter the profession as a money-making business . . . while in the rank and file of the profession he will be very poorly paid . . . he cannot hope to leave the ranks until he is nearly thirty years of age, but before that he may possibly secure a salary of £300, or £400 per annum; still on entering the profession and for no short period of his early life he can only calculate on earning a few guineas a week. Although there are many public appointments in which the remuneration exceeds £1,000 most can only in exceptional circumstances expect to make more than £700 or £800 and the difficulties facing a young man entering upon private practice are great.[16]

In 1885 Mr D. E. Mills, in his retiring address 'Fifty Years of the Liverpool Engineering Society', ended with some comments on professional training. 'The special facilities for acquiring attainments for the engineer,' he said, 'are nothing like what they should be.' Sir William Fairburn, said Mills, speaking to the Manchester Mechanics' Institute thirty years previously, had said that Britain must produce for future service a more intelligent and better-educated class of foremen, managers and workmen. But the Mechanics' Institutes, the Atheneums and the Lyceums had failed to serve the particular classes for whom they were originally intended.

Therefore we are still in want of institutions and museums for the scientific and industrial tuition of the artizan class . . . the necessity for technical education has become greater than ever. The old idea that a 'practical man' was worth two 'theorists' is now exploded; the two must go hand in hand. The young engineer must not be disheartened by the weariness caused by a long fatiguing day of manual labour, nor deterred from prosecuting his studies in his evenings and spare time.[17]

Again, in his retiring Presidential Address in 1887 the President, J. W. Webster, chose to speak on 'Technical Education'. He said:

We are told that other nations had for many years past devoted

85

themselves to the scientific training of their population . . . that unless we quickened our paces in the direction of practical scientific and technical education of the masses we should 'fall into the rear more and more'.[18]

This was not so, he claimed. The income of the Department of Science and Art, which was a mere £1,500 in 1853, was by 1887 over £400,000. Also there was the City and Guilds of London Institute which had an annual income of £40,000. We spent more than any other country on imparting technical education to the masses, said Webster. Our workshops were the finest technical schools in the world and had produced Watt, Stephenson and Armstrong, and with regard to the arts of construction England was still top. We were the naval architects of the world and were pre-eminent in iron and steel manufacture.

The President in 1891 was Professor Hele-Shaw and he returned to the theme of education. Hele-Shaw began by pointing out that the ways of becoming an engineer were manifold, for engineering embraced civil, mechanical, electrical, mining and marine engineering. He then reviewed the ways in which some of the leading engineers had entered the profession. Sir William Cubitt, the son of a miller who built the first two landing-stages, had joined a firm which made agricultural implements; this had led on to windmills and thence to harbours. Mr Charles Fox, who constructed the roof of the Crystal Palace, had first been articled to a medical man, only to give this up and go in for railway engineering. Charles Vignoles had begun his career by studying law but then went in for railway engineering and eventually became the first professor of civil engineering at University College, London. Sir William Fairburn had been apprenticed at Percy Main collieries and Sir Joseph Whitworth had joined Messrs Creighton's works at Manchester. Henry Bessemer had come to London at eighteen and got work as a designer. On the other hand, the only two foreigners on the list had both received a university training.

Times, however, had changed, Hele-Shaw pointed out. At one time an engineer was a many-sided man who could do everything, but now they were becoming increasingly specialised. It was the common practice of large works at this time to keep apprentices at one branch or detail of a branch. The artisan was therefore at a disadvantage, for the introduction of new machinery superseded his acquired skill and there were few opportunities for an artisan to go further. As befitted an ex-Whitworth Scholar, it was natural for Hele-Shaw to mention Whitworth's scheme. In 1889, said Hele-Shaw, not one of the Whitworth Scholars was still an artisan, although the scholarships were really open to working men. Apart from such openings as these and evening classes, another important means of education for the young pupil was through joining a professional society. The Institution of Civil Engineers, which began in 1830 with 191 members, by 1890 had 5,872 members. The same picture was presented by the Institution of Mechanical Engineers and the Institution of Electrical Engineers.

One of the most stimulating papers presented to the Society was that by J. B. Jeffrey in 1915 on 'The Education of a Marine Engineer' and this provoked a lively discussion. Jeffrey had pursued a course of technical instruction in Germany and had served an apprenticeship at one of the largest shipbuilding yards in Germany. The war would throw the Germans back, but he rightly predicted that the Germans would recover and rely on British dilatoriness to overtake them. According to Jeffrey, the German engineer lacked the adventurousness and inborn inventiveness of the Britisher but education had made the German an engineer; what he lacked in mechanical genius he made up for in education. After these introductory remarks Jeffrey outlined the paths to a career as a marine engineer in the two countries, and this is best summarised by the following sketches.

(a) GERMANY

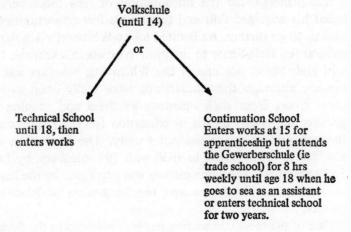

Volkschule
(until 14)

or

Technical School
until 18, then
enters works

Continuation School
Enters works at 15 for
apprenticeship but attends
the Gewerberschule (ie
trade school) for 8 hrs
weekly until age 18 when he
goes to sea as an assistant
or enters technical school
for two years.

(b) BRITAIN

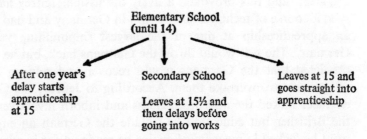

Elementary School
(until 14)

After one year's
delay starts
apprenticeship
at 15

Secondary School

Leaves at 15½ and
then delays before
going into works

Leaves at 15 and
goes straight into
apprenticeship

The British scheme of training often involved delays before leaving school and entering into apprenticeship; also the German apprenticeship system was far more vigorous, the apprentice being placed at a bench between two trained mechanics.

Mr Thomas Thomas opened the discussion by posing the question 'What education does a marine engineer get?' In his view it was very little—only sufficient to pass the very low standard of the Board of Trade examinations. He had himself been an examiner and was appalled at the low standard of examinations—yet 60 per cent had failed in Liverpool the previous year. The majority of engineers went into workshops at fourteen or fifteen with little ground work and little of value in the way of technical education done for them. 'Evening classes', said Thomas, 'were no good because boys lacked good basic education.'

Mr Lloyd Barnes announced that Cammell Laird had, at his instigation, developed a bonus scheme for apprentices. The foremen were told to aid the apprentices in attending the technical school and if at the end of the first year at technical school the apprentice obtained good marks in mathematics and physics his apprenticeship pay would go up by 2s a week for the four years. It had been suggested that the classes should be in the day not evening; but Lloyd Barnes did not think this was necessary. He had a grudge against the universities, for 90 per cent of those who obtained scholarships never returned to the works—after three years at University they got better positions in teaching than they would get in engineering. This was hardly a logical condemnation of universities—rather it was a reflection of the state of the engineering profession.

Mr Booker, who was not himself a marine engineer, was surprised to find that the training of marine engineers could hardly be said to exist in Liverpool, and that the universities and shipowners apparently took little part in the matter. Mr Booker seems to have been in ignorance of the existence of the Liverpool School of Naval Architecture (established 1892) and it is astonishing that throughout the discussion there was no mention of this school.

Mr E. G. Forber wished that he had been born forty-five years later, for when he was a lad he had to start work at 6am and finish at 5pm, only to have to go home to Walton and get back to his classes in Shaw Street by 7pm. He was able to follow the teacher up to a certain point, beyond which he might as well have stopped away for the rest of the course. The request had been made to many Liverpool workshops that those who attended night classes should not have to attend work before breakfast the following day. This worked very well with those firms that complied with this, and men worked harder as a result.

The difficulties facing the young apprentice a half-century earlier as outlined by Mr Forber had changed little according to Mr B. G. Orford. An engineer apprentice rose at 5am to be at the shop by 6am. He reached home tired by 6pm, washed and dressed and was back at his classes by 7 or 7.30pm, where he listened to two lectures if he could keep awake. He left at 9.45pm and was home at 10.15pm to snatch six hours sleep. This he did on three evenings a week—on the other evenings he did home-work, for even if he passed the examinations he would not receive the certificate if he had not done sufficient homework. Education should not be made unduly difficult, only to be obtained at the cost of injury to one's health. Employers, he thought, ought to require the two-year diploma course of a trade school from apprentices.

Although he was unable to be present, Mr A. E. Laslett sub-mitted his views by correspondence and they agreed with these earlier speakers. His recollection of the system in vogue thirty years previously was not pleasant. There were long arduous days in the shops followed by three or four hours at the technical school, where the blackboard became gradually more and more dim to the sleepy eyes of the tired student. This system resulted in partially educated young men who had no chance of making good the weakness of their educational equipment. The remedy, he wrote, was with employers and educational powers. He strongly pleaded for day-release schemes—it was a long time before these were to be implemented. In his report to the Mosely Education Committee, Mr Robert Blair, the Chief Education Officer of the London Education Committee, asked: 'Are we not putting an unnecessary severe strain on our very best material? In these days of international and industrial rivalry, can we afford to allow the "lad o' parts" to sacrifice so much to the process of "coming through"?'[19]

Many members had pointed out that the standard of the Board examinations was abysmally low, but Laslett claimed that the Board's members had wanted to raise the standard of the examina-tion, but were prevented by the total failure of the educational bodies to raise their educational standards. Most engineers who presented themselves for certificates looked on the process of cramming and sitting for the examination as a necessary in-convenience to be endured in the effort to get promotion and so more pay, with no thought of taking the opportunity to equip themselves better.

According to Mr McLachlan, Day Technical Trade Preparatory Schools were in an experimental stage in this country. Extensive research work was needed in engineering and in education—the administration of education was carried out in a haphazard fashion. He went so far as to claim that the evening-class system was based on the survival of the fittest and on the further principle of 'throw plenty of mud and some will stick'.

As a result of his experience as a chemistry student at Tübingen and Strasbourg, Mr G. C. Thompson was of the opinion that the German engineer did not have the same adaptability and resource in a difficulty as did the British. At Tübingen he found that students who came from the technical college to obtain a PhD were not as resourceful as the university student and both were behind the British.

Mr Willet Bruce put his finger on a real weakness when he pointed out that in Britain the boy who went to sea as a marine engineer did so through 'sheer accident', whereas in Germany the boy had a definite purpose in view. For instance, in a Hamburg shipyard employing 150 apprentices the larger proportion of the boys knew within twelve months of the termination of their apprenticeship in which company's ships they would make their first voyage.

This debate was conducted only a few years after the rediscovery of Mendel's work on genetics and the impact this made on learned men of the time is evident in the discussion. There was misunderstanding over the meaning of inherited and acquired traits; many speakers referred to 'our hereditary instinct for engineering', while others argued that it was an 'acquired instinct'. Professor W. H. Watkinson said that 'this country had relied on our hereditary instinct for a long time. The Germans, however, were gradually getting that instinct and in addition they received a far superior training.'

Although, as we have seen, there were widely divergent views among the members as to whether or not Britain was industrially on the decline, there was complete unanimity of opinion about the necessity for an improved system of technical training. Many speakers thought that the subject needed more attention than it had been given previously and all agreed that it was of vital importance.

Although papers were read on a wide variety of engineering subjects, the two major themes that speakers returned to again and again were 'technical training' and 'industrial prosperity'. The President during the session 1912–13 was Professor Watkinson and he devoted his Presidential Address to these most topical of questions, and his views can be taken to be representative of opinion prevailing immediately prior to the outbreak of war. In 1910 he said 264 million tons of coal were mined in Britain, 202 million tons of which were used for home consumption.

If the whole of this 202 million tons had been converted into coke or coalite, it would have been possible to obtain from it 20 M.tons of tar and from this 8 M.tons of tar oil suitable for use in Diesel engines and this would give power equivalent to 32 million tons of coal. Since the weight of coal used in British ships in 1910 was $21\frac{1}{2}$ million tons it is evident that we might, in this way, obtain more than all the oil required for the propulsion of all our ships. When this revolution in the methods of using coal is effected, we shall warm our houses by coalite, by gas or by electricity.[20]

Watkinson then followed this introduction by outlining the development of the diesel engine.

Engineering is both an art and a science, and, in the past, development in the art has usually preceded the science of the subject, i.e. the practical man has produced the new engine or machine, and afterwards the science of the subject has been developed. This order is now being reversed, and the scientific treatment of the subject is preceding the development of the art of construction of the new machine. The development of the diesel is an example of this. Diesel investigated the problem from the scientific side before proceeding to have engines constructed, and he adopted the unusual course of writing a scientific treatise on the subject at the time his trial engine was under construction. This method of investigating the scientific aspect of the problem before beginning the constructional part has the great advantage that it, in general, saves a great deal of money, which under the older system had to be spent in making costly trial and error experiments.

We in this country, have, in the past, attached greater training in the art than in the science of engineering, and in consequence we have not been so well fitted as the Germans to develop those branches of engineering which are more dependent on scientific knowledge. The following examples will serve to illustrate this point. The high-lift turbine pump was invented by Professor Osborne Reynolds, but Continental engineers have, owing to their better scientific training, developed the high-lift centrifugal pump, also the water turbine so much beyond what we have done, that our manufacturers lacking the knowledge necessary for the design of these, have, in many cases, had to buy the designs from Continental firms.

The two-stroke cycle gas engine was invented by Dugeld Clark in 1880, but the development of this type of gas engine was left to Korting of Hanover and the application of this cycle to Diesel engines is being developed in other Continental countries. All the big internal combustion engines, whether using gas or crude oil, which are being built in this country are German or Belgian designs, for which our manufacturers have to pay tribute.

The application of Diesel engines for marine propulsion has been entirely developed on the Continent, and the many British firms now beginning to build these engines are doing so from Continental designs and with the help of Continental engineers.

The large steam engine was first rendered successful by Parsons but the study of the scientific side of the subject was at once taken up in Germany and in Switzerland, and when I was in Berlin four years ago, I was humiliated to see enormous steam turbine plant being built for South Africa.... Not only are the Germans sending their steam turbines to South Africa, but they are also sending them in increasing numbers to this country, and even to Newcastle, the birth place of the steam turbine. Many of the large steam turbines being built by British manufacturers are Continental and American designs. It is the story over again of the aniline dyes, but now applied to many branches of engineering.

Our manufacturing engineers appear to have been so deeply impressed by the superior knowledge of Continental engineers in the departments referred to above that they have been afraid of adopting inventions and designs of British origin.[21]

At this point Watkinson turned to the problem of technical training. He began by quoting Sir Swire Smith, who once said:

Our future as a manufacturing country depends more than ever upon our industrial leaders; are they being sufficiently trained? Here are some facts that should give us pause. In engineering, chemistry and technology there are two technical High Schools in Germany and one in the U.S., in each of which there are more students above the age of 18 taking three year courses than are to be found in all the technical schools of the U.K. put together.

Watkinson continued:

A large proportion of our manufacturers and other employers have not yet learned to utilise highly trained men to the extent that these are utilised on the Continent and in America. Foreign firms have learnt how to utilise large numbers of technically trained men in their works. It is said that for every ten artizans in a plant there is at least one highly trained expert, and that works employing 1,000 men will have a staff of at least 100 men who have been trained at Technical High Schools or university. It is the business of these men to do the thinking, planning, designing and experimenting. . . . During the last 30 years engineering science has developed enormously and it is no longer possible to obtain adequate training for the higher branches of the profession by attendance at evening classes. The time available, especially for laboratory work, is far too short to enable the more advanced branches of the work to be properly carried out. . . . Our evening classes are better than those in any other country, and their great success has tended to obscure the necessity for the fuller training which can only be obtained in day courses.[22]

Watkinson was again returning to the familiar theme of 'evening classes'. He cited an address by Mr Charles Washburn, delivered at Worcester Polytechnic Institute, Massachusetts, in 1906. In this address Washburn drew attention to the too great emphasis given to the value of 'evening classes' in England and its resultant effect.

These night-schools are exceedingly common in England, so common that they have undermined the influence of the regular day schools, and have implanted the erroneous idea into the mind of the average young Englishman that he can work all day, go to school at night and still be successful in each case. . . . The Germans

94

have not made this mistake and emphasise the necessity of giving undivided attention either to educational work or to industrial work, but not to combine the two. . . . When the Americans awakened to the need of better scientific training for their engineers, they did not come to this country, but to Germany, to find their models for schools of engineering, and nearly all their great schools of engineering which have been built up in recent years, are founded mainly on the German system.[23]

Watkinson supported his argument by quoting figures to demonstrate the rapid expansion of engineering in the United States. Between 1902 and 1908 the number of universities and higher colleges which taught engineering had exactly doubled, increasing from 13 to 26, and the number of engineering students had more than doubled, increasing from 8,239 to 18,186. In Germany in 1909 there were 10,998 students in the Technical High Schools, the great majority of whom were taking the regular diploma and degree courses, in addition to which there were a further 5,000 who were not qualified to work for the diploma. In the universities and technical schools of England and Wales there were only 1,623 full-time engineering students, 20 per cent of whom were under eighteen. Watkinson concluded his address by pointing out that the laboratories in the US and Germany were on a scale far beyond any that were available in the UK and that in all the universities and technical high schools abroad research was being carried out.

In his retiring address of 1886 Coard Pain, the President, took as his theme 'The Depression of Trade as Affecting Engineering'. He could find no single satisfactory cause for the depression of the mid-1880s. Commerce was paralysed, confidence in all financial operations was shaken and industrial stagnation ensured. We no longer held the comparative monopoly of the iron trade that we had so long enjoyed and due to the enormous volume of trade still being carried out we had been tardy in realising the strength of those competing. Mr R. R. Bevis, in his Presidential Address of 1884, described the events of local engineering importance. The most significant of these had been the Manchester Ship Canal, which a Committee of the Houses of Parliament had

95

estimated would save £1 million per annum. By this time, too, the Mersey railway tunnel had been completed between White-chapel, Liverpool, and Market Place, Birkenhead. Important de-velopments had taken place in ocean steam navigation, best average speeds doubling from 9 knots to 18 knots during the period 1840 and 1884.

Between 1875 (its first year of true operation) and 1913 the membership of the Engineering Society grew from fifty-one to over 600 and during that time there had been thirty-six presidents. It is of interest, however, to point out that among all these names there were only six who appeared to have graduate qualifications—this is in strong contrast with the Physical Society. The six to whom this applied were Robinson Souttar, MA (Oxon), President in 1878; M. E. Yeatnam, MA (Cant), 1879; Professor Hele-Shaw, DSc, 1894; John Brodie, MEng (Liverpool), 1898; A. Bromley Holmes, MEng (Liverpool), 1899; and Professor W. H. Watkin-son, MEng (Liverpool), 1912.

The obituary notices of the Society reveal the path by which most members entered the profession in those days. Sir William Henry White (1845–1913), who was an honorary member, had entered the docks as apprentice at the age of fourteen. Thomas Duncanson (1852–1913), an engineer to the Liverpool Corporation Water Works, who had helped in the construction of the Vyrnwy Dam, had been educated at Liverpool College and by private tuition, and later served a pupilage under Thomas Duncan and Alexander Duncanson, Water Engineers to the Liverpool Corpora-tion. Joseph Price (1844–1913) served an apprenticeship in mechani-cal engineering with Messrs T. & T. Vicars and completed his technical education at the Mechanics' Institute. He started business as an ironmaster at Workington where he was one of the first users of concrete; he later returned to Liverpool, taking over the Brunswick Foundry. George Hyde (1868–1912) was trained in the engineering department of the Great Northern Railway Company.

The Engineering Society was the largest scientific society in Liverpool and one of the wealthiest. Its receipts in 1912 were £443, of which £440 was raised by subscription. £150 of this was spent on the publication of the Society—the *Transactions*. As well as being concerned about productivity and technical training, members devoted much attention to a wide range of engineering problems, and numerous papers were read on railways, docks, harbours, electric lighting, propellers, steel manufacture and house drainage. The interest in engineering was also catered for by the *Liverpool University Engineering Society Journal*, the first volume of which appeared in June 1912. In this first issue two papers of interest were 'Prospects for Civil Engineers in Canada', by A. J. Cowie, BEng, and 'Function of the Laboratory' by Professor E. W. Marchant of Liverpool University. Cowie thought prospects were good in Canada, where universities and engineering colleges worked hand in hand with large industrial concerns. Engineers in Canada were infinitely superior to their English counterparts at the end of their courses because they had received a total of two years' experience.

Professor Marchant's article was based on a paper read to the Liverpool Engineering Society and Manchester Section of the Institution of Electrical Engineers on 18 November 1911. As far as he knew, an engineering laboratory was first established by Professor Kennedy at University College, London. He went on to say:

> Laboratory work appeals especially to the English temperament, which is experimental rather than theoretical. . . . In spite of this fact the laboratory has reached its greatest development in Germany and America, largely because the funds that have been available for educational purposes have been much greater as a rule than they have been here. . . . The laboratories in Berlin, Dresden, Carsruhe and some other places, can hardly fail, at first sight, to cause a pang of envy in the minds of those who have to work with far fewer facilities.[24]

From these discussions taking place amongst the engineers of the Liverpool region during the late nineteenth century and early twentieth century it becomes apparent that the profession was far from indifferent to the problems of education and training. Nevertheless, in the field of engineering education Germany and the United States had much to teach Britain, and less to learn from us. The failure to establish an adequately trained engineering profession at this time in Britain can be traced to a number of root causes. Besides the early engineering talents being practical rather than educated men, Britain had failed to take note of the gathering momentum of the second Industrial Revolution during the late nineteenth century. Unlike the first Industrial Revolution of the eighteenth century the second was built on a foundation of highly trained and educated manpower. The sort of talents that had initiated the first were felt in England to be adequate for the second, and the Germans and Americans proceeded to demonstrate that this assumption was invalid.

British engineering not only suffered from outdated attitudes towards education and training, but also from the low status of the professional engineer. Much of the leadership in the engineering field of the first Industrial Revolution had come from the working classes (eg Richard Trevithick and George Stephenson), and it continued to be viewed as a profession for the bright young man from 'the lower orders'.

By the late nineteenth century effective decisions in the field of education and training had to be taken at a national level. The voice of the engineers was not strong enough to persuade the various governments of the time to make the right sort of decisions regarding educational provision for the profession, and on the right sort of scale.

The engineers in Britain seventy years ago were well aware of the training and education problems facing the profession, but were unable to implement adequate solutions. Such discussions as those recorded here for the Liverpool area led to piecemeal initiatives, often taken at a very local level. Despite the progress made since World War II many of the problems remain.

From: *Annals of Science* (June 1971), Volume 27, no 2

6 The Education of the Industrial Worker: the Cornish Mineworker—A Case Study

Introduction: the Decline of the Cornish Mining Industry

The presidential address to the Royal Cornwall Polytechnic Society in 1895 included the words 'I am sorry that I cannot speak in eloquent terms of the future of Cornish mining'.[1] For the last thirty years of the nineteenth century Cornwall was indeed dominated by the decline in mining activity in the County.

Mining throughout the nineteenth century in Cornwall was sensitive to the international and national economic climate. The 1837–45 trade recession, which hit Britain badly, was particularly harsh in its implications for the Cornish:

> A great number of our miners are now working on the railways or wherever they can procure employment: and several of them are selling their little cottages and preparing to emigrate to Mineral Point in North America, in quest of that productive labour so necessary to the support of themselves which they cannot now obtain in Cornwall.[2]

The assisted passages offered by the Government for those emigrating to Tasmania and South Australia aided those wishing to leave the County. The Australian copper and Californian gold discoveries of the 1847–9 period saw Plymouth and every port in Cornwall prospering through the emigrant ship trade. The local newspapers were full of reports such as the following from the *Royal Cornwall Gazette* for 9 April 1847: '. . . upwards of 700 persons have left Camborne parish within the last 10 days for Australia and North America'. In three months of 1849, 3,690 persons emigrated from Plymouth for Australia, and 1,058 in a single week for Quebec.[3]

However, prosperity returned to the Cornish mines in the 1850s. In 1854 the County had 19,292 employed in copper mining, and 14,131 in tin.[4] But in the following decade cheaper copper from Chile and Michigan led to the Cornish mining slump of 1866–7. The County's production of copper ore had been worth £816,582 in 1861, but by 1871 this had dropped to £205,025. This was the end of Cornwall as a major copper producer; as the *Royal Cornwall Gazette* reported in its issue for 2 January 1868, '8,000 miners have recently left Cornwall in search of bread, having 20,000 persons dependent on their energies'.

A tin boom followed in 1870–2 but was short-lived. The value of tin production was £1,246,135 in 1872, but the County's earnings had fallen to £530,737 by 1878. Forty-seven mines closed in 1874, forty-eight in 1875, and thirty-seven in 1876. The opening of the Suez Canal, in 1869, aided the European import of Malayan and Australian tin. There were other factors which functioned to the detriment of Cornish mining:

> For centuries past Cornish speculators had been interested in tin, and the industry had developed in such form as to give control to a comparatively small group of metal smelters. These men had often been interested in copper as well, and when the Cornish copper mining industry collapsed in the panic of 1866 they sought other fields for mining investments; since so many of them already made quite considerable investments in overseas copper mining ventures they were quite prepared to speculate in foreign tin mining as well.[5]

The late 1880s and early 1890s saw European capital being poured into the alluvial tin workings of Malaya, which were aided by the introduction of hydraulic mining. Malayan tin production doubled between 1887 and 1894. Malaya was further assisted by the abolition of silver as a monetary standard in Europe; the European value of the Straits' silver dollar declined from 3s 8d in 1879 to 2s 1d in 1894. The Malayan mine-owner paid his men in silver but sold his tin for gold. The Federated Malay States' output was 25,911 tons of tin in 1890 and 46,983 tons in 1894. Greater world production of tin brought the price down to

£38 per ton in 1895, which made Cornish output uneconomic. Cornwall had produced 37 per cent of the world's tin output between 1861 and 1870 (world average of 24,000 tons per year), but between 1891 and 1900 only 9 per cent (world average of 77,000 tons per year). Cornwall had produced 15,157 tons of black tin in 1863 but only 5,659 tons in 1899.[6]

From his work the miner gained a bare living, which even in the better years had to be supplemented by keeping a small-holding. In 1838 the average wage was £2 12s 6d per month,[7] whereas by 1879 a miner would earn 15 to 16s per week.[8] The Depression, which began the decline of Cornish mining in the 1870s, made emigration inevitable, but it was also considered a welcome change for some:

> It is not too much to say that between the Census of 1871–81 a third of mining population of Cornwall left the County. The Registrar-General in his Report on the Census of 1881, says that the population of Cornwall had decreased by 8·9 per cent, and that it is probable that the miners diminished by 24 per cent.[9]

Such was the initial impact of the mining decline. The emigration of the best of the miners made the Cornish industry even less competitive. Those who were left, both in management and as miners, were remarkable for their conservative attitudes:

> Dolcoath and Tincroft had tried these (i.e., rock boring machines) in the late 1860's but Doering, their great pioneer in Cornwall, was reported to have been laughed at by other mine adventurers for his pains and even to have lost a great deal of money in endeavouring to convert the conservative Cornish miners from the old slow hand boring.[10]

The exodus from Cornwall provided an abundance of talent in other countries both in mining and elsewhere:

> A long line of Cornishmen entered the American (Methodist) ministry; no less than 46 of those who served in the Californian Conference are said to have emigrated from St. Agnes parish alone between 1859–1909.[11]

Emigration was not confined to the labouring classes, skilled or otherwise. This was a characteristic of the professional classes also. Opportunities for acquiring training and skills in the mining industry were limited and often the way to the top was through practical experience rather than qualifications and education, as was the case on the Continent. Throughout the greater part of the nineteenth century the leading mining institution in the country was the Royal School of Mines. In the next section of this paper it is seen that students trained at the School of Mines found it more expedient to enter mining abroad and hence were just as likely to emigrate as were the practising miners, although perhaps for different reasons.

Mining Education

In 1835 Sir Henry De La Beche, Director of the Geological Ordnance Survey of Great Britain, suggested to the Chancellor of the Exchequer the idea of a Museum of Economic Geology. This was opened to the public in 1841, and pupils received instruction in analytical chemistry, metallurgy, and mineralogy. A new building was opened in 1851 and at the inauguration De La Beche announced:

> It has been deemed expedient to extend the lectures so as to embrace instruction of a character resembling that given in foreign schools of mines, and, while it should be adjusted to the wants of the country, should also have reference to the mineral wealth of the Empire at large. . . . It would be needless to point out the bearings of mining schools of France, Saxony, Russia and Austria, upon the mineral resources of those countries—the useless expenditure they prevent, and the real productiveness they provide.[12]

This was in line with the report of a committee of the House of Lords in 1849 which observed:

> Among those best qualified to speak upon the point, a want appears to be felt of facilities for acquiring mining education, such as are provided by the mining schools and colleges established in the principal mining districts of the Continent, apparently with the most beneficial effects.[13]

This move had been precipitated by a growing demand among the principal mining districts urging the establishment in Britain of an institution similar to the mining schools which had long existed in France and Prussia. As a result, the Museum was reorganised into a School of Mines and of Science Applied to the Arts, and lecturers were appointed in geology, mining and mineralogy, applied mechanics, practical chemistry, metallurgy, and natural history. During the first session the attendance was most disappointing, there being only seven bona-fide matriculated students and those mining districts which had pressed for a mining school having sent not a single pupil. Dr Lyon Playfair, who was lecturer in chemistry, pointed out that pupils came up with a consequent loss of time in their having to learn the elements of science instead of its applications.

In 1855 the Director, De La Beche, died and was replaced by Sir Roderick Murchison, who saw, or thought he saw, the advent of a time when the scientific character of the Institution under his charge would be dealt with by men who had no knowledge of, or sympathy with, science. He wrote to Lord Stanley, Lord President of the Council, pointing out that the School had been founded to bring science to bear upon the productive industry of the country, with a view to the development of its mineral wealth:

> Liberal as the minister may be under whose control the general education of the nation may be placed, there is little doubt that in this country the greater number of its instructors will be drawn from among such of the graduates of the ancient universities, as, both by their training and position, must be to a great extent disqualified from assigning their due importance to the practical branches of science. Such persons may be eminent in scholarship and abstract science, and yet ignorant of the fact that the continued prosperity of their country absolutely depends upon the diffusion of scientific knowledge among its masses.[14]

The School of Mines was the only large and comprehensive mining institution in Britain during the nineteenth century, though attempts were made to establish similar schools at Wigan, Cornwall, Glasgow, and Bristol. But even at the Government School of Mines the annual average of matriculated students (ie students who entered the full course at the School) during the first two decades of its existence was only fifteen.

Although the mining industry was fundamental to the economy of the country, it did not acquire professional respectability until the end of the century, when the Institute of Mining Engineers was created in 1889 and the Institute of Mining and Metallurgy in 1892. Graduate status was not achieved until the twentieth century, when London instituted a BSc (Engineering) in Mining and Metallurgy, and Newcastle a BSc in Mining. Only a handful of graduates had been produced, however, by the time World War I broke out.

Meanwhile, HRH the Prince of Wales as Duke of Cornwall had granted two exhibitions, of £30 each, to matriculated students of the Royal Government School of Mines. Few graduates of the School returned to the Cornish mining area.

A survey of the records of the former students of mining of the School reveals that some 55 per cent of them entered mining abroad mainly in South Africa, Australia, India, and North America.

Of those remaining in Britain 17 per cent became lecturers or teachers and only about 10 per cent entered mining in various capacities; these included mine managers and consulting mining engineers. Former students of the School also became principals of the Cornish mining schools at Camborne and Penzance.

The general pattern of education throughout most areas of the country was well illustrated in Cornwall, where the grammar schools did little to further the education of the working artisan classes and the education they offered the middle classes was narrow in outlook and restricted in range.

For instance, Launceston Grammar School in 1867 had a school population consisting of twenty-seven boys. The upper boys were reading Caesar and Virgil. Two had begun algebra and a few could do fractions; several of them did simple sums correctly.

Their knowledge of geography was small. Some of them were fairly acquainted with English grammar. The boys were principally taken from the sons of the chief tradesmen of the towns, interspersed with a few sons of professional men and farmers. The boys generally left young, often at thirteen.[15]

Poor as things were at Launceston, in the rest of Cornwall the position was immeasurably worse. At Bodmin, for example, the grammar school of the capital town of Cornwall had shared the fate of many similar schools in the country and had ceased to exist. Liskeard Grammar School was discontinued in 1849, and Penryn Grammar School had closed by 1867. At Fowey the Grammar School was considered to be no better than an elementary school.

The 1870 Education Act saw the Government taking part in educational provision on an unprecedented scale, but this was only an answer to the continuing problem of illiteracy. There was a need to make miners more competitive in the effectiveness of their labour through greater educational facilities of a vocational type. Cornish mining interests increasingly appreciated that to counter the challenges from places such as Malaya the disadvantages, such as deep mining and more expensive labour, had to be made up for by greater efficiency and the most modern concepts. Unfortunately, the efforts made in provision, whether local or national, were inadequate and belated. In Cornwall the most ambitious provision, a combination of private initiative and some public funds, was that of the Miners' Association:

> In the autumn of last year, you are aware that another combination for a similar purpose was made under the auspices and through the influence of Mr. Hunt. It was entitled the 'Miners' Association'. . . . It is proposed that Mr. Pearce should work in those several districts in connexion with the Miners' Association . . .
> The difficulty in the way of success has chiefly arisen from the indifference of miners themselves to this species of knowledge.[16]

In these terms the Royal Institution of Cornwall introduced the readers of its *Report* in 1860 to a significant new creation in the field of Cornish vocational education, its aid to the new institution in the form of the services of Mr Pearce, and what has always been a problem for those involved in such provision, viz the indifference of the clientele.

There had been previous attempts to form an institute to carry out the functions in which the Miners' Association was particularly interested. For example, in 1844 there had been the Miners'

Society based on Redruth: 'the plan of which society appeared to be an association of practical men, familiar with the details of mining, and with the construction of machinery, who will meet for that interchange of ideas, which must have a great tendency to promote their objects.'[17] But the Miners' Association was a better-planned creation, which appeared at a good moment in Cornish mineral development, and which served the whole County. Very quickly the Association had all the trappings of success:

> The Miners' Association . . . can now boast of 200 subscribers; subscriptions to the amount of £250 per annum have been already secured. Four classes are at work (St. Just, St. Agnes, Lostwithiel and Tywardreath), and other districts are anxiously asking for the services of our teacher. I trust, immediately after the general meeting, we may be in a position to appoint a second teacher.[18]

The aim of the Association was 'simply that of educating the miner' (General Honorary Secretary Robert Hunt, FRS)[19] and 'thereby to aid in the improvement of a great industry, which contributes to our national wealth about £3,000,000 per annum, and to relieve the producers of this treasure from many of the baneful influences which attend them in their subterranean toils'.[20] In this there is a characteristic Cornish middle- and upper-class approach found during the nineteenth century of wishing to combine greater economic efficiency with an improvement in the intellectual welfare of the working classes.

The Quarterly Meetings of the Association gave an opportunity for ideas and suggestions to be aired, and possibly for agreement to be made regarding future action on such proposals. A Quarterly Meeting held at Camborne on 16 April 1863 thrashed out the whole question of the educational provision for miners.[21] The attendance was small and consisted of J. F. Basset of Tehidy in the Chair, Enys of Enys, Messrs Cady and Simmons, Captain Charles Thomas, Captain John Tonkin, Captain Lanyon, Captain Phillips, the Educational Secretary Richard Pearce, and the General Secretary C. Twite.[22]

Captain Tonkin started the discussion by suggesting that evening schools should be opened for miners to improve themselves in writing and arithmetic, and thus be prepared for the better appreciation of the (Association) instruction afforded by the lecturers.[23] Tonkin was making an appeal on behalf of the miners whose education had been neglected, but Chairman Basset was out of sympathy with the idea as he felt it did not come within the sphere of activities of the Miners' Association, there already being schools in existence.

Tonkin estimated that 'three fourths of the young men now working in our mines are destitute of this elementary knowledge [of writing, reading, and arithmetic]'.[24] This figure, although high, was confirmed by Pearce. The reasons for this Tonkin explained as follows:

> Most of our young working miners leave school at ten or twelve years of age; afterwards, scarcely any of them attend a day or night school, and by the time they are twenty, they have probably forgotten nearly the whole of what they had learnt.[25]

Although there was much sympathy with Captain Tonkin's viewpoint, Cady indicated one of the major difficulties facing the Association in establishing night schools for miners, viz that the society had a debt of £207.[26] Cady also pointed out that greater teaching demands could not be made upon their lecturers, who were already overworked.

Captain Charles Thomas[27] read to those present a paper he had prepared on the education of miners. In this he established the sort of content a training programme would have for the practical miner. It included a study of mineral veins, the opening of a mine, surveying, extraction of ores, mechanical engineering in relation to the steam engine and pumps, mineralogy and assaying, and the dressing of ores. But Thomas took such training a stage further, with the miner educated in moral and religious principles.[28]

To enable the miners to take advantage of such courses Thomas wanted the opening of evening schools in every town and considerable village in the several mining districts on three nights a week to teach the first principles of all education—reading, writing and cyphering.[29]

As an institution which might serve as an example he quoted the Wesleyan Evening School (at Camborne) with pupils numbering:

... 93, 70 of whom are miners from the age of 13 to 23 years, and two of 11 years old. This school is open three evenings in each week free of charge, the teachers being paid from funds raised by private subscription etc.; the pupils pay for the books, paper etc.[30]

Although he was advocating a considerable increase in the educational provision for miners, Thomas observed that:

... to say that every miner should be educated would be ridiculous, as it was not needed, and another thing [was that] it would be useless to attempt it, as there are some persons who could not be instructed. They were intended for workers and workers they would continue to be.[31]

By the standards of the day, Captain Thomas was one of the foremost advocates of working-class education; if he felt some miners would gain nothing from tuition there must have been a more conservative element in positions of authority who were suspicious of educating anyone not of the middle and upper classes.

This particular Quarterly Meeting is a useful example, as it demonstrates both the character of such occasions and the attitudes of many of the leaders of the Association to the whole question of working-class education. Although the Meeting was not exclusive regarding those entitled to attend, only a very small group of mining leaders came, whilst there was no representation of the recipients of the work of the Association. Although much scathing criticism was levelled at the work of the Association,[32] it might have been more fruitful if the views of the working miner had been heard.

The education of miners as seen by the Association referred to those endowed with intelligence, rather than even the working classes of average ability. An élite amongst the miners appears to have been the aim of the Association. Such a group would ensure a pool of talent to improve the efficiency of Cornish mining in an increasingly competitive international field. Fundamental education such as reading and writing provided by evening schools was to be a tool to bring the intelligent miner to a stage of development whereby he could benefit fully from the courses provided by the

Association. Universal education was a concept of little interest to many of the leaders of the Cornish mining community.

Despite some criticism from its members the Miners' Association was considerably encouraged by the time of its Third Report (1863). The Council recorded that they felt they had:

> ... every reason for believing, from the eagerness for the acquirement of knowledge exhibited by our miners, that there is amongst the young working miners of Cornwall and Devonshire a very earnest desire to learn something of the sciences which they feel will aid them in their labours.[33]

By 1863, classes were being held in St Just, St Ives, Helston, Redruth, St Day, St Agnes, St Blazey, Crow's Nest (Liskeard), and Gunnislake. This was considerable progress for a society which had seen the first classes established a mere two years previously.

In 1863 there were 200 persons studying under the Miners' Association teachers, of whom 118 were working miners.[34] The rest of the classes consisted of the agents, assayers, and mine clerks. To broaden the appeal of the work of the Association, the teachers (Hunt, Pearce and Twite) also gave lectures of a popular character, the subjects bearing directly on mining and mineralogy.[35] These were well attended, with some audiences numbering more than 100 people, mainly miners.

The reports from the various centres illustrate some of the strengths and weaknesses in the provision of the Miners' Association. At St Agnes a twenty-meeting class attracted only an average of nine students; the sessions were devoted to '... the analysis of the different ores, their chemical and blowpipe characters, assaying by the wet and dry methods, the nature and use of fluxes etc.',[36] which may have proved rather too functional and intellectual a diet for the intelligent miner. In defence of the small attendances it should be pointed out that this was the first year of such classes being held at St Agnes.

Twite's classes at Redruth struck problems as the working miners did not attend, whilst the middle classes gave considerable support.[37] In the same *Report*, Robert Hunt levelled similar criticisms at the Mechanics' Institutes:

One objection that presents itself is that the Mechanics' Institutions of Great Britain are not at the present moment institutions for the benefit of the working men of Great Britain. They have passed into the hands of a higher class, and we consequently feel that if we were to join them, we should not, through the Mechanics' Institutions as at present constituted, reach that class which the Association is intended more particularly to benefit.

To condemn Mechanics' Institutes as lacking working-class support and then to find mainly middle-class audiences attending the Association classes at Redruth caused some embarrassment.

The picture at Helston had been a happier one, with classes averaging from fifteen to twenty students, composed mainly of miners.[38] Both Pearce and Twite taught at Helston, which may have provided variety as an added attraction. The subject which seems to have caught the imagination of the miners at Helston was chemistry, for which purpose they had provided themselves with books on the subject, for their private reading. However, all was far from perfect even here. A familiar problem of modern adult education was the much-voiced complaint that attendance during the winter months was affected by bad weather.

At Liskeard the twenty-three members of the class had been engaged in collecting metallic ore specimens which were to provide the basis of a local museum.[39] In Gunnislake, meetings took place twice a week under the supervision of Captain J. Cook.[40] One evening was given over to the practice of dialling and arithmetic and the other to lectures and reading on subjects useful to miners. The lectures were given by various members of the class, which had a total of twenty and an average attendance of twelve. Gunnislake demonstrated the limited professional teaching resources available to the Association. The experiment in using class members was an interesting borrowing from Mutual Improvement classes, but was most successful when one of the teachers was present.

The often poor support which the early efforts of the Association received was a matter for concern amongst the patrons of the society. In an age somewhat less liberal in its approach to the working classes the solutions suggested were direct. F. H. Trevithick's bald statement represents such an approach: 'I would suggest that the working miners of Cornwall must be brought together, and I would go as far as to say that this should be done by force, if it cannot be otherwise accomplished.'[41] The suggestion was not taken up, but further incentives were developed as an alternative.

Perhaps the greatest incentive for many of the more intelligent miners came in 1863 with the Association's decision to join the Government's Department of Science and Art scheme.[42] The lecturers of the Association became certified teachers of the Department, and those members who had attended classes on forty occasions were entitled to present themselves for examination in May of each year. The Royal School of Mines offered scholarships to those who passed exceptionally well the Department of Science and Art's examinations. These examinations were to be the mainstay of the Miners' Association for the rest of the century, and represented for the miners the primary provision for part-time study leading to qualifications in his field.

The success of the Society in tuition was impressive, as appears from the following testimony:

> It may be well to call attention to the fact that of the nineteen candidates (Science and Art Department) throughout the whole United Kingdom in Mineralogy more than [one] half received their instruction in the classes of the Miners' Association.[43]

A year later there was elation when a working miner succeeded in winning the Gold Medal in Mineralogy of the Department of Science and Art, which meant that he had come top in the United Kingdom.[44] The Gold Medallist was given £10 by the Society of Arts to visit the Paris Exhibition.[45] The Association's educational provision not only was of a calibre equal to that of any other mining district in the United Kingdom, but success in the examinations could bring a miner benefits of considerable attraction beyond the experience of most members of the working class.

The Association not only provided teachers but also books and apparatus for a modest charge.[46] There is little doubt that there was amongst the miners a minority who found the Association's provision of value, and took full advantage of it. Even allowing for an understandable bias in the *Reports*, there is plenty of evidence to support the belief that a sizeable working-class demand existed; for example:

> The earnestness with which the young men in the several classes are proceeding with their studies cannot be more convincingly shown than by the fact that they have recently, chiefly at their own cost, provided themselves with the books, which, at the trade prices at which they are supplied to the Association, have cost nearly £30.[47]

A rapidly increasing demand led the Association to bring in a scheme whereby from 1868 onwards the more advanced pupils taught classes in their home neighbourhood. This meant eight classes under instruction, as against three in 1867.[48] In 1867, forty-nine Department of Science and Art certificates were gained by the Association's pupils,[49] and in 1870 this figure had increased to eighty-four.[50]

Successes increased as the Association improved its organisation and built on the earlier foundations. 'During the past year two of the men belonging to the Carharrack class, J. T. Letcher and S. Mitchell, were successful in gaining the prize of £20 offered through the "Mining Journal" for the best Essay on mining tools and machinery', proudly recorded the Association's *Report* for 1872.[51] By 1876 the number of passes in the Department of Science and Art examinations had reached 207, but this figure masks further triumphs: 'Of Queen's Medals, the only one awarded for Mineralogy, one of the two given for Steam and one of the four given for Inorganic Chemistry, were received by students in the classes of this Association.'[52] The society was at this time running twelve classes with 242 students.

In 1878, organisational changes took place within the Association.[53] Due to the rapid development of the system of teaching in district units, plus the growth in the number of certificated teachers trained in the society's classes, it was decided that any class offering the subjects recognised by the Miners' Association could become affiliated to the society on payment of an annual fee of not less than 5s. Also, classes in the Districts were to be to a greater extent self-supporting. These changes aimed at increasing the Association's work whilst at least partly combating the ever-present problem of limited finances. By 1879 the Association's debt had been paid, and the students had gained 304 passes in the Department of Science and Art examinations.[54]

The 1889 Technical Instruction Act and Further Developments

Despite the fluctuating fortunes of Cornish mining the Miners' Association provision continued to prosper. In 1890 it could be stated that:

> the educational branch of the Society's work has made great progress. In Camborne and Redruth the numbers of students attending the schools have been greatly increased. At Penzance new schools, on a large scale, are in the course of erection. At St. Just two large classes have been established this session. All round there are abundant evidences of a growing desire on the part of young miners and artizans to avail themselves of the advantages offered by the various schools and classes.[55]

Whereas other adult education institutions within Cornwall found themselves being replaced in their roles as the century progressed, the Miners' Association was able to take advantage of new legislation being passed by Parliament. The 1889 Technical Instruction Act permitted County and Borough Councils to levy a penny rate for technical and manual instruction. This was a good principle, but the cost of establishing the intermediate schools in Wales or the technical schools in England was high, and they might never have come into being except for the most extraordinary series of chances.

> In 1890, in the hope of encouraging temperance, a Bill was brought in raising the duties on spirits, and appropriating some of the resultant money to compensate publicans whose licences were to be extinguished. The proposal for compensation met with the most determined opposition. The debate waged for twenty-five days, and at last the Government were glad to accept a compromise proposal that the 'whiskey money'—otherwise called the 'residue' should be given to the County Councils to be used—if they saw fit—

for education. If they did not wish to use it for education they might use it to reduce rates. . . . In England, tentatively at first, and then more boldly, it was used for technical education in the towns and for agricultural schools in the country.[56]

All over the country, County Councils and County Boroughs were loath to raise a penny rate, as they were entitled to under the 1889 Act, and in 1892 only eleven authorities were doing so, but most authorities devoted 'whisky money' to technical education. In Cornwall no rate money was spent on technical education, but £6,000 of the local taxation finances was made available for it.

The Association was quick to see the significance of 'whisky money' in relation to its own activities, and began lobbying the County Council. At the Annual Meeting on 19 February 1891, the position of the Association was clearly expressed:

It is hoped that a substantial portion of the Fund at the disposal of the Cornwall County Council will be allotted to the Mining Association and Institute for the further promotion of Technical Education under the auspices and direction of the Society.[57]

The Association was not unduly disappointed by the County Council's response; for example, in 1894 it was recorded that:

. . . the County Council have further assisted by another grant the work of the Society in connection with the museum, and have officially intimated that they approved of the methods adopted to make the museum as useful as possible in the furtherance of technical education.[58]

The Museum had been created as a memorial to Robert Hunt, who had died in 1887, and it had been opened in 1891. The building consisted of a hall of 40ft by 30ft, with rooms underneath for the caretaker and for storage.[59] The Redruth Literary Institution lent its mineral collection to the Robert Hunt Museum,[60] and generous contributions came from other societies and individuals in the County. The Museum represented a further stage in the creation by the Miners' Association at Redruth of a complex of facilities. Rooms had been built in 1883 from private donations totalling between £1,200 and £1,300, and with a grant from the Department of Science and Art at South Kensington of about

£500.[61] The resulting Institute had set a precedent which was followed by the Association in the creation of schools in other areas of Cornwall. Because it provided technical education for miners and artisans, and with a leadership ever ready to take advantage of favourable legislation, the Miners' Association did not face either a crisis in finance or in its role within society during the nineteenth century.

With such facilities available, the examination results of 1891 were impressive, with 336 passes recorded among the Association's students.[62]

The membership of the Association did not decline in the latter part of the century. In 1885 the Association had 188 members, one honorary member, and eight annual subscribers (mainly mines).[63] By 1887 this figure had increased to 243 members, ten annual subscribers, twenty associates and thirteen teachers.[64] The teachers were those who taught the affiliated classes of the Association. During the 1890s the Association further improved its membership position, with 300 members, forty associates, and eighteen teachers in 1894.[65]

Conclusion

In 1859 the creation of the Miners' Association was initiated by a resolution moved by Charles Thomas, and seconded by G. Fox, at a meeting chaired by J. St Aubyn, MP. Perhaps the most significant of the innovators had been Robert Hunt. This creation partly fulfilled such an obvious gap in the education provision of Cornwall at the time that it continued to grow in strength throughout the rest of the nineteenth century. Its main contribution was in making teaching facilities available to help those intelligent workers who wanted to gain qualifications in the examinations of the Department of Science and Art field, or similar examinations. But it also had many ancillary contributions to make to Cornish adult education. It ran educational excursions for its students, beginning modestly with places of mining interest within the County, such as Chiverton in 1867,[66] and later travelling much farther afield, as was the case in 1890 when the trip was to South Wales.[67] In 1873 the *Report* mentions the existence of a Circulating Library,[68] which must have been a considerable benefit to the studying miner in 1885 when the Mining Association and Institute Medal was established.[69] It was awarded to students who had worked at least twelve months underground as miners, and had first-class passes in the advanced stage of the 'Principles of Mining', and any two other of the recognised subjects. In awarding the Medal, a first-class ordinary stage in 'Ore Dressing' in the City and Guilds of London Institute Technological Examination was considered equivalent to a first-class advanced certificate awarded by the Department of Science and Art.

Perhaps the achievement of the Association is best summed up by the example of one of its students. 'The Basset Mines group was formed in January 1896 with a nominal capital of £100,000 under the guidance of Francis Oates, who was the largest shareholder, together with the Bolithos of Penzance. Oates, originally a working miner from St Just who had been a star pupil of the Miners' Association "migratory" or travelling schools . . . had emigrated to South Africa in 1874, where his mining skill raised him to the day-to-day control of the Kimberley diamond mines and to a directorship of the huge De Beers combine.'[70] The educational opportunity afforded by the Miners' Association to working-class pupils of ability like Oates made it a major institution in the history of nineteenth-century Cornwall.

It was a characteristic example of the kind of local effort made to bring technical education to the artisan and mine manager. The work of the Royal Cornwall Polytechnic Society and the Royal Institute of Cornwall and other bodies forms a similar pattern. By the standards of the day these were very commendable and worthy attempts to fill the gap created by the absence of State initiative and provision. In the last analysis, however, they were inadequate substitutes for a properly organised, State-subsidised scheme of technical education.

From: *Paedagogica Historica*, Volume XI, no 2, 1971

PART III
SELF HELP

7 Private Enterprise and Technical Education: the Royal Cornwall Polytechnic Society

The Founding of the Royal Cornwall Polytechnic Society

In 1833 the Cornwall Polytechnic Society was established at Falmouth 'to stimulate the ingenuity of the young, to promote industrious habits among the working classes, and to elicit the inventive powers of the community at large'.[1] Probably the name was suggested by the École Polytechnique in Paris and represented the first use of such a title in Britain.

Members of the Fox family of Falmouth[2] were the primary movers in the creation of the Polytechnic Society. In the eighteenth century, George Croker Fox had established himself as a shipping agent and merchant in Fowey. He came to Falmouth in 1759, and in 1762 the firm of George Croker Fox & Company began business as consuls, ship agents and merchants. By the beginning of the nineteenth century the family had a reputation for producing intellectuals of some standing. One of the most talented was Robert Were Fox, a man of considerable scientific attainments and a Fellow of the Royal Society. He had two daughters named Anna Maria and Caroline, who were brought up within a small but highly cultivated community. It was the enthusiasm of these sisters, whilst still in their 'teens, which led to the establishing of the Polytechnic.

In 1791 the Fox family had set up the Perran Foundry at Perranarworthal, the first major ironworks within the county. The elder sister, Anna Maria, was impressed by the fact that the workmen of the Foundry kept coming to her father with inventions and suggestions regarding their work, and felt the inventiveness of the workmen should be encouraged by some institution to serve the demands of the situation. In 1833 the time was ripe for such a suggestion and few societies can have had a smoother birth, mainly due to the support given by the local gentry. During the nineteenth century support came from most of the County's famous families, such as the Bassets, Vyvyans, Lemons, Enys, St Aubyns, de Dunstanvilles, St Levans, Pendarves, Williams, Robartes, Borlasses and the Foxes. Their enthusiasm is perhaps not surprising when one reads the aims of the Society in its early years:[3]

> ... [the Society] by furnishing such a stimulus to exertion, would create an honourable spirit of emulation, not only among scholars but among the conductors of schools, and would afford them the means of profiting by each other's improvements . . . it would develop capacities and talents which would otherwise lie dormant, and bring into notice many useful improvements that but for this means would remain unknown . . . it would afford to seamen an opportunity, and hold out to them a stimulus, to employ their leisure time in long voyages, in executing plans or models of nautical improvements, and also excite some interest in collecting the natural curiosities and mechanical contrivances of foreign countries.

Lord de Dunstanville was the Society's first patron and Sir Charles Lemon its president. There were ninety-eight subscribers, each of whom was asked to pay 5s. From the beginning an annual exhibition was to be held 'for the purpose of displaying productions of arts and industry'.[4] Members or other interested persons were asked to loan for the exhibition 'any specimens of science and art, ingenious contrivances displaying thought either in the principle or in the execution, natural curiosities, or other objects of public interest'.[3]

The Distribution of Prizes
Prizes were to be offered at the annual exhibition for scientific and mechanical inventions and improvements, work in the 'fine and useful arts', and for good workmanship. Many of these prizes aimed at improving the state of mining in the county. Among the first offered[5] was one of 10 guineas by Charles Fox for the best improvement of methods of ascending and descending mines. At the same time, Sir Charles Lemon and R. W. Fox offered 10

guineas 'for the best series of practical experiments, tending to prove how the dangers attendant on blasting rocks may be most effectively and economically guarded against'. Besides the importance of mining economically there was a belief that 'the miners are an ingenious class of men, and from their habits, and the nature of their occupation, thoughtful and reflecting'.[6] Similarly there was ever the vision that:

> ... the genius of a Watt has, perhaps, often slumbered within the breast of many a rude and uneducated mechanic, whom poverty and neglect have led to mistrust his own powers. The germ of thought has either been repressed in the bud; or may have expended itself in crude and hopeless attempts; or in the pursuit of some chimerical project, for want of some fostering hand to prompt his endeavours, and direct his energies into the right channel.[7]

This vision was to remain with the Society for much of the century, and in the leaner years of the 1890s was probably a factor in causing the Society to exempt the 'working classes and persons under 16 years of age from the entrance fee of three shillings'.

Encouragement of the 'working orders' brought immediate success, with prizes awarded at the first Exhibition to Richard Hosking of the Perran Foundry for the invention of a water gauge for steam boilers, and a lathe for cutting screw tools. Other prizes were awarded for oil, watercolour and pen and ink painting, for charts and maps, fancy work, models of known machines, and a category described as 'miscellaneous' where a Mr N. Tresidder gained recognition for his 'Glass Birds' Eyes'.[8] Greater success came the following year with Michael Loam of Consols Mines being awarded the prize for ascending and descending mines with an idea based on 'the principle of balanced rods, working with a reciprocating motion in a shaft, with platforms affixed to them at regular intervals'.[9] Loam's invention, called the 'Man Engine', was tried out on 5 January 1842[10] at the Tresavean Mine. The Polytechnic Society had agreed with the Tresavean adventurers to pay £300 towards the expense of the first 100 fathoms, and an additional £200 when the second 100 fathoms was completed. In fact the Man Engine system was taken down

121

to 290 fathoms (ie 1,740ft) at a cost of £1,312 13s or about £4 10s 6d per fathom. The Man Engine proved most successful and was later used in other deep mines in Cornwall.

The comparative success of the Society can be illustrated by taking an average year like 1842 and listing the major medals and prizes awarded during the Exhibition.[11] Silver medals went to J. Phillips of Tuckingmill for a collection of specimens 'illustrative of the decomposition of rocks and minerals'; Captain Tregaskis for 'an instrument for measuring the velocity of the [steam engine] piston in every part of the stroke'; Mr Rouse for 'a mode of converting the motion of a pumping engine into a circular motion for drawing ores'; J. Reynolds for a 'machine for extending broken limbs'; W. George for 'a dipping needle'; T. Ward for a 'steam coach for common roads'; R. Q. Couch for a paper 'on the development of the frog, and on the sponges'; and two silver medals were also awarded in the water colours painting section. Amongst other prizes awarded were ones for the following: a plan for 'relieving the kibble from the weight of the back chain'; 'an examination for a steam boat engineer'; 'an instrument for setting off the angles of refraction'; 'a method for teaching arithmetic'; 'an improved lock'; 'a mode of converting parallel into circular motion'; and 'a plan for strapping steam engine boilers amidships'.

Writing in the report of the Society for 1869, Charles Fox was able to list among the achievements of the Polytechnic in its first thirty-five years the awarding of nearly 1,000 silver and bronze medals, and £4,000 in prize money. The original design of the medals had been commissioned from Wyon, the chief engraver at the Mint,[12] but the popularity of the awards seems to have declined after 1866,[13] when it was decided, at the discretion of the committee in each instance, that the medal could be converted into money (first silver medal, £5; second silver medal, £3 10s; first bronze medal, £2; second bronze medal, £1 5s).

Growth of the Society
After the death of Lord de Dunstanville in 1835 the Polytechnic became associated with the royal family. King William IV became the Society's new patron, and in 1834 the Duchess of Kent and

Princess Victoria became patronesses. After 1837 Queen Victoria was the patroness of the Society for the rest of the century. The 'Royal' Polytechnic Society, as it became in 1835, saw a rapid increase in its membership. The original ninety-eight subscribers, which included seventeen members of the Fox family, became 374 members[14] (including nineteen Fellows of the Royal Society) by 1836. There were 350 members[15] by 1849, which increased slightly to 368 in 1857 (twenty-three Fellows of the Royal Society),[16] and in 1887[17] there were 278 subscribers within the county, thirty-nine resident outside Cornwall, eleven life members, and four mines held membership. By the close of the century, despite the Queen and Prince of Wales remaining as patrons, the Society was past its golden age, with only 244 members, including nine honorary ones.[18] Because of the subscription required for membership the Society remained predominantly a middle-class institution with its leaders recruited mainly from the local gentry.

The leadership of the Society was vested in the office of President, from 1833 to 1867 Sir Charles Lemon, but after 1868 the post could not be accepted by the same person for more than three consecutive years. Sir Charles Lemon, the second baronet, was born in 1784, and educated at Harrow and Cambridge.[19] Although most of his wealth came from mining, he found time to be MP for Penryn (1807–12 and 1830–1), Cornwall (1831–2) and for West Cornwall (1832–57). He was a Fellow of the Royal Society from 1822, and a founder of the Statistical Society in 1834. From 1843 to 1863 he was Provincial Grand Master of the Freemasons of Cornwall. Amongst his other activities before his death in 1868 was that of Commissioner on the 1847 enquiry into the British Museum, special Deputy Warden of the Stannaries, and author of a number of pamphlets. The influence of Lemon on the Society in its formative years was considerable. Lemon was followed by Lord St Levan, and for the rest of the century the president of the Polytechnic Society was invariably a member of the gentry or nobility.

Exhibitions
Exhibitions were held in the Falmouth Classical School until

123

1836, when the building plans of the Society reached fruition and the Polytechnic Hall was opened. This has been the centre for the Society ever since. The permanent home appears to have benefited the annual exhibitions, as admission receipts increased from £46 in 1835 to nearly £100 in 1837.[20]

At the exhibitions public lectures were given. In 1846[21] the exhibition was kept open for five days, with people allowed in on the last four days for twopence. 'The total number of visitors was certainly not less than 3,300.' During that time those attending would have heard the following papers read: R. B. Fox, 'On the means of lessening the risk of growing potatoes'; R. W. Fox, 'On the high temperature of the water of the United Mines'; G. Bartlett on his fossils; J. Olver, 'Design for a suspension bridge adapted for a railway'; and the Society's secretary on 'Faraday's research on the magnetic condition of all matter'.[22] In 1870 there was a chance to hear E. B. Tylor on 'The relation of primitive to modern civilization'; F. E. Fox on 'Arctic Regions'; J. H. Collins on 'Natural phenomena'; J. Macgregor on his Arab travels '. . . concluding with a specimen of Arab music, which seemed to electrify those present'; and finally, J. H. Collins on the 'Sun, Moon and Stars'.[23]

At the exhibitions the county was often introduced to new inventions of considerable importance. At the 1877 Exhibition 'The Mechanical Department . . . included the Telephone, for which the Society is indebted to Professor Graham Bell of Boston, through whose kindness this Society was enabled to bring that highly valuable instrument for the first time before the general public in this County. The instrument was worked in the Hall for 3 days, and by its means communication was held with Penryn Post Office, a distance of over 2 miles'.[24] Such pioneering was highly successful, but had its disadvantages; 'when, however, the telephone was put into communication with Professor Bell's electric organ arrangement at the Post Office, everybody in the Hall was enabled to appreciate its wonderful power, for the tunes were disturbingly audible in every part of the room'.[25] Amongst other inventions demonstrated by the Society at its exhibitions towards the latter part of the century were the electric telegraph, electric lighting, wireless and oil engines. Hence, the Society fulfilled a role whereby the advances in science in particular were communicated to a much broader public than they might otherwise have been.

In the well established tradition of Cornish institutions of the nineteenth century the Society felt a need to found a museum. In 1842 it was reported that 'your committee hopes that when the value of such a museum as the one your Society contemplates, shall be more generally known, donations of the required kind will be presented and that the Polytechnic Hall will become to the County a place of reference for specimens of the manufactures of the kingdom'.[26] The Museum of Economic Geology was never of primary importance, as its lack of mention in the annual reports illustrates, but a small collection was available within the Polytechnic Hall.

The Importance of the Secretary

From the Polytechnic's viewpoint the men who occupied the post of general secretary were of over-riding importance. Those who filled the post of secretary were often talented young men of working-class origin, many of whom became of some eminence in their respective fields later. Robert Hunt, secretary 1840–5, is a useful example for illustrating the Polytechnic's role as a nursery for talent:

> Equipped with only a slender education, he came to London before he was thirteen years of age, and, having secured an engagement as assistant to a medical practitioner at Paddington, rapidly acquired a knowledge of pharmaceutical chemistry. . . . In consequence of illness young Hunt was induced to seek a change of scene, and returning to the West of England undertook a walking tour through the county of Cornwall, collecting with eagerness the legends of the peasantry, and thus acquiring the materials which, augmented by subsequent research, enabled him many years afterwards to write his Popular Romances of the West of England. . . . In 1840 he was appointed Secretary of the Royal Cornwall Polytechnic Society. . . . Mr. Hunt also investigated the influence of coloured media on the germination of seeds and the growth of

125

plants. . . . It was mainly in recognition of such researches that Mr. Hunt was elected into the Royal Society. In 1845 . . . Mr. Hunt was appointed Keeper of Mining Records at the Museum of Economic Geology, in succession to Mr. Thomas Jordan (Secretary of the Royal Cornwall Polytechnic Society 1835–40). . . . When the Government School of Mines was established in 1851 Mr. Hunt had assigned to him the Lectureship in Mechanical Science . . .[27]

Although this is a sampling of Hunt's achievement over many years, it does also indicate the attraction which the secretaryship had for rising talents, and the Society's willingness to employ such men for comparatively short periods.

Not only was the general administration of the Society in the hands of the secretary, but he was one of the mainstays regarding lectures. At the annual exhibition the secretary would frequently give more than one paper, and also demonstrations and explanations of certain of the more interesting exhibits. The place of lectures was virtually guaranteed in a Society which aimed 'to foster and encourage, though in a less systematic form than under a well-devised educational discipline, the spirit of scientific research among our mining population; to reward, to the extent of their abilities, the productions of rising genius, and thus, by concentration and publicity, to give effect to energies, which would otherwise be expended to little or no purpose'.[28] The secretary was periodically called upon to deliver a course of lectures for the enlightenment of both the Polytechnic's members and those who might also benefit (eg the miners),[29] and its popularity made strenuous demands upon the Society's secretary.

Other Educational Activities
Although the policy-making of the Society during the nineteenth century appears often to have been in the hands of a few, the efforts on behalf of the rest of the community were genuine. Encouragement was given to many who might not otherwise have had opportunities to develop interests and talents. The members sat willingly to listen to lectures given by the bright workman: 'Mr. Moss, the intelligent foreman of that part of Messrs. Harvey's works where these facts occurred, was present to read a paper on

the subject'.[30] There was concern to bring to light the conditions under which the working class lived, and to improve such conditions.

With the ability to think in terms of the whole of Cornwall, the Society's exhibition often represented the first recognition of a working-class talent in some small village. The annual reports provide a number of examples, such as the following: 'Alfred Harry, a young man, a mason of Mullion, who last year obtained some encouragement from the Society, for wood carving, has since then made so much progress in modelling, as to receive a first bronze medal, and to secure for himself an improved position as an artist.'[31] In the same year as Alfred Harry's progress was recorded this very point about remoteness was made to the members of the Society: '. . . the utility of this Society, not only in fostering a love of art, but in giving stimulus and opportunity to those who would otherwise, perhaps, never have been able to display their ability, beyond the narrow limits of a county village.'

In addition to catering for the interests of the whole county, there was a breadth to the pursuit of adult education which ranged from the possibilities of instruction of females to the encouragement of meteorology. The latter was of considerable interest to many of the members, and the early efforts at recording the weather led in the 1860s to approaches from the Royal Society and the Board of Trade with regard to establishing a meteorological station.[32] The site for such an observatory was fixed at Bowling Green in Falmouth and building began in September 1867. A lease on the house and the observatory tower was granted to trustees of the Society for a term of twenty-one years from Christmas 1867, at a rent of £60.[33] The observer was Mr Lovell Squire (a former secretary), whose salary was to be met from a Government grant which also covered rent and incidental expenses. Initially, the observations made were of atmospheric pressure, air temperature, evaporation, and the direction and velocity of the wind. The results were published in the annual reports, and also later in the *Western Morning News* and the *Western Daily Mercury*.[34]

Such services, despite outside financial aid, were comparatively costly: 'a statement of the Observatory accounts to 31st December 1877 is presented to you, which shows an adverse balance of £29 13s. 4d. including estimated liabilities. Application has been made to the Meteorological Office for an increased grant, but at present without success.'[35] Like every other similar institution in Cornwall in the last century, the Polytechnic was frequently embarrassed by its failure to match finances to ambitions. However, by 1885 the observatory building programme was completed despite an increasing debt.[36]

The Society also generously encouraged evening classes, aided by the Department of Science and Art. 'The free use of the large committee room has been granted as in several years past for the Science and Art evening classes' the *Report* for 1888 recorded. The following year further endeavours were reported:

> Attempts had been made to develop classes for education as well as for the annual exhibition, and they might look forward in the near future to some further effort being made in the development of Art and Science classes, if not directly in connection with that Society, yet so far in relation to it that the products of such classes might form a large and important contribution to the exhibition held there. They had already in Cornwall some Science and Art classes which were in flourishing condition, and at Camborne there was a Mining School, thanks to the liberality of Mr. Basset and the public zeal which animated the people of Camborne and Redruth.[37]

The Impact of the Technical Instruction Act

The Technical Instruction Act of 1889 was considered to be particularly germane to the aims of the Society by its President, Courtney. As the report for 1889 records, he was at pains to explain to the Polytechnic's members the content of the legislation. The Society was prompt in taking advantage of the possibilities afforded by the Act. It was reported in 1891 that 'classes were now under the conduct of masters appointed by the Technical Instruction Committee, and were attended by a large number of students. Arrangements were also in hand for establishing agricultural classes in the neighbourhood, and dairy classes would be opened at Penryn, where similar subjects would be taught to those which had proved so successful during the past week at St. Germans.'[38] Despite these efforts, a year later the Chairman at the annual meeting (Colonel Tremayne) was urging the Society to give greater encouragement to the Technical Education Committee for Cornwall.[39] The Polytechnic responded by offering medals and prizes at the annual exhibition of 1894 for outstanding work by students in classes conducted by the county's Technical Instruction Committee.[40] This offer of medals and prizes was repeated in following years.

With such encouragement the report of the Falmouth District Technical Instruction Committee[41] for 1894 noted that 246 students had registered for science and art classes, of whom 144 entered for the various examinations, with an end result that seventy-nine gained certificates or other recognition by the Department.

The association between Cornwall's Technical Instruction Committee and the Royal Cornwall Polytechnic Society in the field of science and art classes was initially a happy one. After all, as Robert Fox had pointed out, 'the object of the technical classes was practically the same as that of the Society'.[42] But the County Council became increasingly independent of the Society after acquiring its own building in the Falmouth area for classes. In contrast, the Society had to ask the County Council for financial aid to help to pay for prizes awarded at the exhibition to members of the classes.[43]

Another project of the Technical Instruction Committee of the County Council in which the Society was involved was that of a Fisheries School at Falmouth. The views of the Polytechnic were sought by the County Council, and a report by the Society was sent to that body and also published in the *West Briton* and the *Cornwall Gazette*. These activities also led the Society in 1894 to persuade associates to contribute £328 14s towards the cost of such a scheme.[44] The outcome of this joint venture was the appointment of Mr Vallentin as 'Lecturer on Fisheries to the County Council'.

In the latter part of the century the Society also gave encouragement to the University Extension movement. At the Exhibition of 1884, R. D. Roberts gave an address explaining the Cambridge University local lecture scheme.[45] However, Cornwall in fact became part of Oxford's sphere of activities. By 1888, Oxford University Extension Scheme lectures were being held under the auspices of the Society, with the use of the Polytechnic Hall granted for the purpose.[46] Although material on the activities of Oxford University Extension lectures in the County is sparse, the example of the Polytechnic Society suggests they fulfilled a demand within Cornwall. By 1890 the Society was reporting: 'the Hall was again let for the Oxford University Extension lectures. This is a boon that is very highly appreciated by those attending these instructive courses.'[47]

The Decline of the Society

Despite its ability to be in the forefront of innovation within the field of adult education, the last quarter of the nineteenth century nevertheless saw the Society in decline. The General Committee[48] found the reason for the Polytechnic's difficulties to be the depression which 'has so long marked the chief industries of the county'. As early as 1848 the tendency of the Society's fortunes to fluctuate with those of Cornwall's economy had been reported, particularly with regard to the mining industry.

Closely allied with the undermining influence of Cornwall's economic problems was the success of the Society in fulfilling many of its original aims, and the replacement of many of its roles by government institutions. In 1872, 'the general education of the community, now inaugurated by the Legislature'[49] had been noted. The beginnings of universal elementary education, the establishment of public libraries, and the activities of the County Council in the field of technical education demanded that the Society modify its role, as indeed it did in the twentieth century, into that of an institution serving the more narrow cultural needs of the Falmouth region.

Rival attractions and a changing social environment made the exhibitions less relevant to the community than they had been at the beginning of the century. The Secretary, Edward Kitto, stated[50]

130

that the Exhibition of 1896 had cost £91 more than the receipts taken, that of 1897 £111 more, and that of 1898 £123 more. The Society's liabilities exceeded assets by £259. From the 1870s onwards the exhibitions had been an increasing financial liability, but it was not until 1898 that it was decided to hold them every two years, a decision which led to an impressive improvement in the Society's finances. 'The result of not holding an exhibition in 1899 was that the funds of the Society were £85 better off than last year.'[51]

Despite its continuing patronage of working-class adult education in, for instance, the provision of the Husband Scholarship[52] at the Camborne School of Mines, 'restricted to Artizans', the Society could not stave off the effects of the economic depression, the migration of Cornishmen, and the taking over of educational provision by state and local government bodies. The words of A. N. Deakin in 1899 held more meaning than he had perhaps intended: 'It must, therefore, be a subject of great satisfaction to the Royal Cornwall Polytechnic Society, on whose behalf I am now speaking, to know that many of the changes which have taken place in recent years have been made along lines laid down by that Society, fifty or more years ago.'[53]

During 1892–3 a suggestion was made which would have been unthinkable in more thriving times, namely that the Polytechnic Society should amalgamate with other Societies within the County. Although this idea was crushed at the annual general meeting in 1893, it would appear to indicate the weakened position of the Polytechnic. Although there was to be no fusion of membership or funds with other institutions, more joint meetings were to be arranged, and 'closer sympathy' was to be the objective. Such aims seemed to indicate a Society much less sure of itself.

Evaluation of the Society's Work
Despite the uncertainty of its role in the changing social circumstances of the latter part of the century, the Polytechnic Society's contribution to Cornish adult education had been the equal of any of the other voluntary institutions within the County. The aims of the Society ranged from that of being 'a convenient channel

131

of communication to the public'[54] to that of hoping 'that the encouragement which we bestow will help to develop talents'.[55] These ambitions frequently met with considerable success. In 1859 the Society indulged itself to the extent of reprinting certain favourable reports found in the newspapers and journals of the day.[56] The *Plymouth Mail* was profuse in its praise: 'We do not think this product of the far west can be paralleled elsewhere in England. Even London's Polytechnic Society was an imitation of it. . . . The intellect and imagination are kept alive by it; invention is stimulated; the most recent scientific discoveries become generally known, and the performances of the higher minds permeate the lower intellectual strata.'

During the nineteenth century the Polytechnic was a Society which stimulated adults of all classes by an exhibition that introduced Cornwall to new ideas and inventions, by the encouragement and patronage of the talented, by its enthusiastic support of other bodies interested in education, by lectures and the annual publication of a journal, by the provision of a reference library, small gallery and museum, and by its ability to grasp quickly the needs of contemporary society and at least try to make some provision for them. Perhaps no more apt summary of its work can be made than Sir Charles Lemon's remark in 1842 that 'the Society addresses itself to all classes of the Community'.[57]

Conclusion

The Royal Cornwall Polytechnical Society failed for a number of reasons. The aims and objects of the institutions were too vague and diffuse and attempted to be all-embracing: '. . . To furnish a stimulus to exertion . . . to develop capacities and talents which would otherwise lie dormant . . . afford to seamen an opportunity and hold out to them a stimulus, to employ their leisure time in long voyages . . . to improve the state of mining in the county . . . to foster the love of art.'

It is little wonder that among all these idealistic and ambitious objects that technical education often took a back seat despite the Society's claims. It was misleading and even something of an impertinence of the Society to adopt the name 'Polytechnic' after the École Polytechnique, for the latter institution was one of the earliest and finest technical schools ever to be erected, attracting the leading French savants as pupils and staff.

Although originally the leaders of the Society were concerned to foster technical education, they were men with no real knowledge of scientific and technical education as practised on the Continent. It is doubtful whether prizes, exhibitions and lectures were the best means of achieving their objects. Further, as the century wore on the hierarchy increasingly adopted middle-class cultural attitudes and technical education was neglected in favour of liberal adult education. As a result, in the latter part of the century, the Society became more and more a fashionable cultural institution and the artisan and working classes were squeezed out. The original Polytechnic Hall is now the Falmouth Arts Centre.

The Society claimed that its failure was due to an industrial depression, but this factor affected equally the Liverpool School of Science and other institutions, which continued to flourish despite adverse circumstances. It can be said in favour of the Society that its efforts, at least initially, were made on behalf of the whole community, but the population was too thin and scattered for it to be able to devote itself wholeheartedly to one line of development. Nevertheless, the truth is that by 1900, with the government and local authorities fully awake to their responsibilities and anxious to take over existing educational provision, or at least integrate them into a clearly defined framework, there was no room for such organisations as the Royal Cornwall Polytechnic Society, which was in the event by-passed by the local authorities.

From: *The Vocational Aspect of Education* (Summer 1970), Volume XXII, no 52

8   Private Enterprise and Technical Education: the Liverpool Literary & Philosophical Society

The Literary and Philosophical Societies were established in the late eighteenth century and the first part of the nineteenth century, the model usually being that of the Manchester Literary and Philosophical Society, founded in 1781. Of them Kelly[1] states: 'It is a development characteristic particularly of the North, and is clearly associated in part, though by no means exclusively, with the new interest in applied science arising from the Industrial Revolution'. They were institutions serving the intellectual needs of the middle classes and the gentry, although they not infrequently gave their aid and patronage to efforts to provide education and training for the 'lower orders'. During the nineteenth century the Literary and Philosophical Societies were to be found in most of the larger urban areas. In 1851 Hudson[2] lists such Societies in the following English towns: Birmingham, Bristol, Hull, Leeds, Liverpool, Manchester, Newcastle, Plymouth, Portsmouth, Preston, Scarborough, Sheffield, Whitby and York. Kelly[3] mentions also those at Halifax, Leicester, Barnsley, Rochdale, Warrington, Nottingham, Bath, Gloucester and Ipswich. There were others also, such as that at Chichester,[4] which were less well known or which were short lived.

From the number established it would appear that the Literary and Philosophical Societies were of considerable significance in the post-school education of the middle and upper classes of nineteenth-century England. That the Societies were committed first and foremost to education can be of little doubt from reading the aims of the founders or noting the content of the annual programmes. The founding of the Leeds Society was stimulated by a letter in the *Leeds Mercury*[5] in 1818 in which the writer stated:

It has long been the subject of surprise to me, and I believe to

134

many others, that although the town of Leeds is justly celebrated for the number of its benevolent and humane institutions, it can boast of no Society for the promotion of intellectual and literary improvement, nor any which might afford opportunities to our youth for the increase of their knowledge, the display of their talents, and the formation of habit as productive of happiness and comfort, as of virtue and honour. . . . I can hardly suppose it possible that any man of reading or sense, can be blind to the beneficial effects of such a society. . . . An acquaintance with history, with languages, and with literature places him in a higher rank in intellectual life, and with men of talent, than any intrinsic advantages however great, and the pursuit of these studies fills up the leisure hours in the most beneficial way because they improve the mind, quicken the faculties, regulate habits, and restrain youth from those paths into which their strong passions and lively habits would otherwise hurry them.

Of the Portsmouth Society, *The Portsmouth, Portsea, and Gosport Literary and Scientific Register* (Thursday, 20 June 1822) wrote: 'Perhaps there is no event which has afforded more true satisfaction to the friends of learning and science, resident in these towns, than the establishment of this Society. Indeed, an institution so adapted to gratify the taste of the thoughtful and enquiring; to arouse and stimulate the powers of the mind; and to provide for intellectual and scientific worth the high reward of notice and commendation: such an institution can scarcely fail to interest the public attention, and to acquire the countenance and support of every person possessed of a liberal and enlightened understanding.' The Halifax Society was created in 1830 following four lectures by a Dr Harwood on the 'Natural History of the Animal Kingdom', which stimulated interest. It was proposed that 'a Literary and Philosophical Society be forthwith formed in Halifax, and that such Society establish in aid and illustration of its objects a museum for the reception of all subjects connected with the various branches of Science. . . . That the Society hold periodical meetings in the Museum for the discussion of Literary and Scientific subjects.'[6] The words introducing the other Societies differ little from the sentiments here quoted. The 'educational vision' of the institutions remained clearly before them throughout the nineteenth century. In 1865 those with influence in the Liverpool Society[7] were stating: 'It should not be lost sight of that the Literary and Philosophical Society is one for the advancement of knowledge, and not for the mere diffusion of learning, and that, therefore, only such papers as can be said to increase the boundaries of science or literature have any claim admitted into its published Transactions.' A president of the same Society had stated in 1857: 'Liverpool has done but little for science, though science has done much for Liverpool'[8].

Besides providing for the dilettante intellectual pursuits of the middle classes and gentry the Literary and Philosophical Societies were established to help the more affluent to adjust to the changes taking place in nineteenth-century England. In an age before the university school of business studies was available, or before such effective mass media as television, these institutions ensured that the middle and upper classes were kept informed both of the developments taking place, and the adjustments they needed to make to come to terms with the new industrial age.

Lecture Programmes and Proceedings
For most of the Societies the core of educational provision was the lecture programme. It is perhaps most helpful to look closely at the programme of one of the Societies during the nineteenth century to gain an effective impression of the work in this area. The Liverpool Literary and Philosophical Society, being neither as eminent as the Manchester Society nor as obscure as the West Kirby Literary Society, provides a good example of an 'average' institution. It was effectively established on 21 February 1812 and was in decline by the end of the century when the *Proceedings* recorded: 'The Council regret to notice this falling off in the number of members elected, and trust that the members generally will endeavour to help the Society by bringing forward suitable candidates for membership. . . . The Council would draw attention to the rule by which Ladies are now eligible at half the ordinary subscription.'[9]

Prior to the publishing of the *Proceedings*, which began in the 1840s, and made available in printed form the more important papers given before the Society, the following list of lectures gives some idea of the sort of subjects dealt with in the early years of the institution:[10]

7 April 1821 'Application of the Malthusian principles to the case of Charitable Institutions'—D. Wylie.

7 December 1821 'Physiological Remarks on certain functions of the Lungs'—Dr Carson.

6 October 1822 'Notice of Mr Scoresby's recent discoveries on the coast of Old Greenland'—Dr Traill.

4 April 1822 'Description of Perkin's Steam Gun'—Rev Scoresby.

7 April 1826 'On the Means of Securing to the Higher Classes in Society, a proper Superiority in Education'—Mr Macgowan.

6 January 1827 'On Absenteeism'—F. Fletcher.

4 January 1828 'On Phrenology'—Mr Grundy.

6 February 1829 'Remarks on Mountain Echoes'—Rev W. Scoresby.

1 October 1830 'On the Standard of Taste, and the Proper Definition of Beauty, in the Fine Arts'—Rev W. Lamport.

6 February 1835 'On Roman Oratory'—Mr Baines.

21 March 1836 'On the Best Means of Promoting the Education of the People'—S. Boult.

26 November 1838 'The Present Social and Political State of Genoa' —R. V. Yates.

22 April 1839 'Proposal for the Improvement of the Channel of the Mersey'—S. Gibson.

2 November 1840 'On the Polarization of the Chemical Rays of Light'—Dr Sutherland.

24 January 1842 'Was the Iliad the work of more than one Author?' —Rev J. Robberds.

6 February and 20 March 1843 'On the Physical Causes of the High Rate of Mortality in Liverpool'—Dr Duncan.

5 February 1844 'On the Chester Mystery Plays'—Dr Hume.

Although one is struck by the diversity of subjects covered in these lectures many of them, such as that 'On Absenteeism', have a very modern ring, and they all reflected the tastes and needs of the contemporary society. As such Societies usually included most of the influential members of the community, the importance of the lectures in getting over ideas and information to the area cannot be over-emphasised. The three lectures given by Dr Duncan are a case in point. The *Proceedings*,[11] when recording his death in the 1860s, make the point well: 'Dr. Duncan, the late medical officer of health[12] for the borough, whose paper *On the physical causes of the high rate of mortality in Liverpool* read before the Society in February and March 1843, and afterwards published, was the means of calling attention to sanitary questions in so prominent a manner, that to it may be distinctly traced the movement which resulted in the passing of that most important act of Parliament usually known as the *Health of Towns Bill*.'

From 1845 onwards, if the members had failed to grasp the educational message of the lectures, they had a second chance with the publishing of the more important papers in the *Proceedings* of the Society, which were brought out annually. To quote the journal itself: 'In conformity with the existing Laws, the general mode of imparting information has been by written Essays on subjects previously announced; and in this form many valuable Papers have been from time to time communicated.'[13] The *Proceedings* also provided a vehicle for publishing papers on the research of the Society's members, such as J. Dickinson's 'The Flora of Liverpool' (166 pages), I. Byerley's 'Fauna of Liverpool' (125 pages), or the Rev H. H. Higgins' 'Synopsis and List of British Hymenomycetes' (105 pages).[14] Such papers could prove an added burden to the Society's finances: for example the larger *Proceedings* for 1851–3 (a biennial edition) cost 4s 6d per copy, whilst the previous one had cost 3s 8½d.[15] During the less prosperous days of the Society the matter of cost led to the passing of a ruling whereby the author had to pay for the printing of any pages of an article in the *Proceedings* after the first twenty-five at a charge of 4s for each additional page.[16]

Not only was the journal of influence within the Liverpool region, but it was dispatched to organisations throughout the world. In the 1880s it was being sent to societies in Amsterdam, Bombay, Bordeaux, Boston, Brussels, Buffalo, Burlington (Vt), Calcutta, Cherbourg, Chicago, Christiana, Coldwater (Mich), Copenhagen, Davenport (Iowa), Geneva, Gireswald, Göttingen, Haarlem, Helsingfors, Königsberg, Leipzig, Melbourne, Milan,

Munich, New York, New Haven (Conn), Otago, Ottawa, Paris, Philadelphia, Salem (Mass), St Petersburg, Stockholm, Strasbourg, Sydney, Toronto, Vienna, Washington and Wellington (NZ).[17] The Society was justifiably proud of this international circulation, noting in 1897: 'The Volume of *Proceedings* published annually continues to afford to the contributors a wide circulation for their Papers, embracing universities, public and learned societies and institutions throughout the world.'[18] Often in exchange for the *Proceedings* the Liverpool Literary and Philosophical Society received the publications of other organisations, so that the members were exposed to a truly international literature.[19]

To show the 'educative' nature of the contents of the *Proceedings* it is worthwhile listing the papers in the edition for 1875–6, which are reasonably representative of the journal:[20]

J. A. Picton, 'The Tendencies and Future of Modern Civilization'

E. R. Russell, 'The True Macbeth'

J. C. Brown, 'On Electricity Compared with Heat as a Source of a Mechanical Power'

Dr T. Inman, 'On a Means Employed for Removing and Erecting Menhirs'

A. Morgan, 'On the Khasi Hill Tribes of North East Bengal, and the Geology of the Shillong Plateau'

J. N. Hetherington, 'On Repetition and Reduplication in Language'

J. Boult, 'Gleanings in the Early History of Liverpool and the Neighbourhood'

T. Ward, 'Salt, and Its Export from the Ports of the Mersey'

E. Nicholson, 'On Indian Snakes'

A. Morgan, 'A Note on Itacolumyte or Flexible Sandstone'

A. E. Nevins, 'On the Method of Correcting the Rate of a Marine Chronometer for Changes of Temperature, According to Mr. Hartnup's Laws, with Tables and Explanation for Facilitating the Computation of the Same Corrections'

Baron Louis Benas, 'On the Men Who Have Influenced Modern German Thought'

J. L. Palmer, 'On Some Tablets Found in Easter Island'

J. A. Picton, 'The House of Stanley and the Legend of the Eagle and Child'

T. P. Kirkman, 'The Janal 14-Acral 14-Edra'
R. Leigh, 'Vegetation and Climate'
W. T. Black, 'Natural History of the Greywing and Redwing
Partridges of South Africa'

Although the growing disinterest of the later Victorian period
in lectures on scientific and technical subjects shows through on this
list, it is nevertheless a remarkable menu to serve the intellectual
appetites of Liverpool's middle and upper classes. As might be
expected there was a steady demand for material of local interest,
whether in the field of local history, or of local commerce and
industry, or regarding local amenities. Some lectures were obviously meant to 'entertain' rather than 'educate'. But a few of
the papers were highly technical and scientific in content. In exceptional volumes the scientific papers were more numerous, as
in that of 1884-5:[21] 'Subjects pertaining to General Literature
formed the topics of seven Papers read at these meetings, and
Science and Philosophy received attention in sixteen.'

Membership and Meetings
The membership of the Society was carefully controlled. There
were modifications of the laws periodically, but the version published in 1850 is representative of the tenor of the regulations
during the nineteenth century.[22] At this time the annual subscription was half a guinea, which should have meant a wider recruitment than the Society experienced, but this fairly modest sum
was not the main factor in gaining membership. The crucial
aspects of application for membership were that the applicant's
form had to be countersigned by two members, and four-fifths of
those attending an ordinary meeting of the Society had to vote
for the applicant. These regulations ensured that only 'gentlemen'
became members. The term 'gentleman' was frequently used
when referring to members: eg 'Any gentleman not residing within
five miles of Liverpool may be proposed as a Corresponding
Member' (ie the bulk of the 'gentlemen' were 'Ordinary Members').[23]

To the categories of Ordinary and Corresponding Members
were added in 1862 two further divisions, those of Honorary

Members (limited to fifty), and Associates (limited to twenty-five). The Associates may have challenged the 'gentlemanly' nature of the Society's membership, but this was an instance of the interests of science being placed before other considerations; the Associates were to be '. . . masters of vessels, and others engaged in marine pursuits, who may have peculiar facilities for adding to the Scientific interest of the Society's proceedings'. Some months later the daring step was taken of permitting women to attend some of the Society's functions: 'The only important change in the conduct of the Society made during the last session, was the passing of a bye-law, providing for the admission of ladies to the meetings on certain occasions, to be fixed upon by the Council'.[24]

Despite, or because of, the careful selection of members the Society was often disappointed with its recruitment. In 1865 it reported: 'The list of the Society, though steadily increasing, has not yet reached that development which we might hope to see in so populous a town.'[25] Probably a number of its potential members found the Royal Institution of Liverpool more congenial. The membership tended to fluctuate. In 1845 there were 135 Ordinary, and sixty-seven Corresponding Members. By 1858 this had become 153 Ordinary Members, and forty-three Corresponding. In 1867 there were 199 Ordinary, thirty-eight Honorary Members, and thirteen Associates. 1875 saw the Society with 220 Ordinary, forty-one Honorary, fourteen Corresponding Members (in West Africa, Ceylon, the Philippines, Honduras, British Guiana, Canada, Chile, New Zealand, and Burma), and seventeen Associates. By 1883 the membership rose to a peak of 258 Ordinary, thirty-nine Honorary, seventeen Corresponding and nineteen Associates. 1891 saw the Society down to 163 Ordinary Members, thirty-two Honorary, twenty-seven Corresponding, and eleven Associates. Although the membership in 1896 rose to 214 Ordinary Members ('The membership has not been so high for many years'), the other categories of membership appear to have been abandoned, and the Society finished the nineteenth century with just 144 Ordinary Members ('the Council urges all members of the Society to bring its claims under the special notice of their friends').[26]

The attendances at the ordinary meetings when papers were

read are also an interesting indication of the dissemination of scientific and technical information. During the latter part of the nineteenth century the *Proceedings* began to record the average attendance at the meetings: in 1881–2 the figure was eighty members; the *Proceedings* for 1893–4 happily recorded: 'There has also been a further increase in the attendance at the meetings, the average having been raised from 70 during the previous section to 95 during that now concluded', and this rose to an average of 111 during 1895–6.[27] From these figures it is perhaps permissible to suggest that the average attendances throughout the nineteenth century at ordinary meetings were high, and occasionally of the order of 100.

The audiences in 1884–5[28] listened to papers on such scientific and technical subjects as 'Observations on the Nematocysts of Hydra Fusca' (R. J. H. Gibson), 'On a New Organ of Respiration in the Tunicata' (Dr W. A. Herdman), 'Technical Education' (F. W. Edwards), 'A Phylogenetic Arrangement of Animals' (Dr W. A. Herdman), 'The Relationship of Palaeontology to Biology' (R. J. H. Gibson), 'Technical Education in England: Its Present Condition and Prospects as Presented in the Reports of the Royal Commissions' (F. W. Edwards), 'Note on the Armature of the Branchial Siphon in some Simple Ascidians' (Dr W. A. Herdman), 'Remarks on Angraecum Sesquipedale' (Dr W. A. Herdman), 'Notes on Coryanthes Maculata' (Dr W. A. Herdman), and 'On the Rocky Mountain Goat' (T. J. Moore). This was a not unimpressive list of science lectures to put before perhaps as many as 100 of Liverpool's more eminent citizens. Although the number of speakers involved was small, Dr W. A. Herdman's contribution being a notable one, the range of subject matter was broad. It would be difficult to envisage a similarly composed modern audience being recruited for such lectures on science and technical studies.

During the nineteenth century the number of ordinary meetings per session varied and were occasionally supplemented by other activities, such as that of 1865–6: 'An experiment has been tried of late, of holding fortnightly social meetings, alternately with the regular meetings of the Society at the houses of various members of the Society who were willing to receive members generally . . . it was distinctly understood, by the gentlemen at whose hands the receptions were to take place, that their hospitality was to be of a simple and inexpensive kind, in order that others might not be deterred from following their example.'[29] Then again the *Proceedings* for 1881–2 record that 'The two Conversaziones in each session, now devoted to Natural Science, are proving to be of great benefit; and the communications then read from the Corresponding Members and Associates abroad show that these gentlemen are making valuable contributions to knowledge.'[30] Although these additional activities tended to be short-lived, or needed to rest on less intellectual foundations (eg 'The Council note with satisfaction the continued success of the Associated Soirées. Eight of these interesting re-unions have now been held, and they bid fair to become a permanent institution in Liverpool'[31]) they could prove to be a supplementary educational experience for members.

The Literary and Philosophical Societies were powerful bodies within their areas, and this tended to work to the advantage of education. They harassed their members in the interests of intellectual pursuits. Societies like that at Liverpool added to the attraction of their educational aims by offering such lures as a 10 guinea gold medal for the best paper read, and by establishing endowed lectureships such as the Roscoe Lectures first given in Liverpool by Professor Max Müller in 1874 on the subject of 'Darwin's Philosophy of Language'.[32]

Other Societies
Liverpool's Society was far from unique in offering its distinguished audiences lectures on such technical subjects as 'Sanitary Reflections, Especially on the Ventilation of the Chimney' (W. Nisbet Esq).[33] The Newcastle Literary and Philosophical Society in 1803 had the Rev W. Turner giving twenty-one lectures on 'Mechanics, Hydrostatics, and Pneumatics', whilst in 1842 the same institution had Mr D. Macintosh lecturing on ten occasions on 'Astronomy and Geology', Mr R. Adams giving twenty lectures on 'Chemistry' and a Mr Sopwith speaking on 'Glaciers'. Even in the 1890s, when tastes were changing, Newcastle (1891–2) offered its members twenty-four lectures on 'Human Physiology'

by Mr E. A. Parkye.[34] The Sheffield Literary and Philosophical Society[35] offered its members, in the best tradition of such institutions, not only lectures but also laboratory facilities, a library, and annual excursions. Many of the Societies followed the nineteenth-century fashion in having a museum attached to their premises, although Liverpool preferred to take advantage of that of another society in the town.

In many ways it is difficult for those born in the twentieth century to appreciate the influence of such institutions as the Literary and Philosophical Societies upon the development of science and technical studies during the nineteenth century. We have got used to a massive participation by government agencies in these fields, and the concentration of resources on organisations such as the universities. But such Societies were of great importance. When the Manchester Literary and Philosophical Society[36] was created in 1781, nearly half its founders were surgeons or honorary physicians to the Manchester Infirmary, so medical science could hardly fail to be influenced by it. Its honorary members included Erasmus Darwin, Benjamin Franklin, Lavoisier and Priestley. Dalton was Secretary of the Manchester Society from 1800 to 1808, Vice-President from 1808 to 1819, and President from 1819 to his death in 1844. During his membership of the Society Dalton read 116 papers. Other famed scientists who were members during the nineteenth century included J. P. Joule (mechanical equivalent of heat), W. Sturgeon (who invented the electro-magnet) and H. Wilde (dynamo, searchlights, and the electro-deposition of copper). Besides offering an eminent audience for the researcher in scientific or technical fields, the Literary and Philosophical Societies often were one of the few institutions providing more practical help in the form of a paid post, or library facilities, or along the lines of Liverpool's initiative in the 1870s when financial assistance was given to the British Association expedition to explore Moab and the area east of the Dead Sea, with two of the Society's members (Rev Dr Ginsburg and R. C. Johnson) making up part of the party.[37]

During most of the nineteenth century the acquiring of some knowledge in the fields of science and technical studies was considered a necessary part of a gentleman's education. Whether the 'gentleman' happened to be of the middle or upper classes such information was usually available to him through the congenial membership of the local Literary and Philosophical Society. The standard of lectures was often of the highest, the membership was influential and frequently intellectually impressive, and the aims of such Societies most laudable. Liverpool's Literary and Philosophical Society saw itself as '. . . a body seeking to foster original inquiry and learned research'.[38]

From: *The Vocational Aspect of Education* (Spring 1971), Volume XXIII, no 54

9 Science and the Amateur: the Penzance National History & Antiquarian Society

In England in the nineteenth century formal education made little provision for a study of the sciences, and an interest in scientific pursuits was inevitably a characteristic of post-school life. The result was the establishing of a number of scientific societies during the first half of the century, such as the Royal Astronomical Society (1820), the Geological Society (1807), the Royal Botanic Society (1839), and the Zoological Society (1826).

Such societies as those listed were serving as national focal points in the sciences, but there was also a local movement throughout England leading to the foundation of scientific societies, or at least the provision of science courses within regional institutions. In the latter part of the century this was to be brought more within the area of governmental provision by the granting of financial assistance under the Department of Science and Art regulations or those regarding the Technical Instruction Acts.

To illustrate the gathering momentum of the local movement in the second half of the nineteenth century it is useful to look more closely at an example of such a scientific society. The Penzance Natural History & Antiquarian Society presents such an example. It is particularly germane as it appears to have been singularly inactive on the 'Antiquarian' side, and to have been neither exceptional nor unexceptional in its provision and attitudes.

The Penzance Natural History & Antiquarian Society was an institution belonging to the last thirty years of the nineteenth century, although it was a reincarnation of an earlier body. In 1839[1] a petition signed by sixty-nine people had been submitted to the Mayor of Penzance, Richard Moyle, which led him to call a public meeting for 20 November. At this meeting the Penzance Natural History & Antiquarian Society was instituted.

The Society lapsed, to be revived in 1862, 'but upon the occasion of removing from its old and elevated quarters in the circular room under the dome of the Market House to the buildings in which we are now assembled [the east wing of the Public Buildings][2], a considerable and necessary outlay was made in fitting up the new Museum, and unhappily it fell into debt'.[3] Under the weight of this debt the Society lapsed once again.

With a well-established middle-class demand for such a society within the Penzance area in 1879–80 'recourse was again had to a requisition to the Mayor . . . to call a public meeting in the hope of once more reviving the energies of the prostrate Society'.[4] The new attempt at revival was successful. The 1880s was a period when such institutions had a popularity that was even greater than earlier in the century; for example in 1887 the Falmouth Naturalists' Society was founded, and had 120 members by 1889.[5]

After 1880 those who wished to become members of the Society had to be recommended by at least two members,[6] and the recommendation had to be placed in 'some conspicuous part' of the Museum seven days before the date of the meeting at which the election was proposed to take place. In the first year members were elected by the Committee, but afterwards 'at ordinary general meetings by ballot'. Candidates could be excluded from the Society by a majority of the Committee voting against their membership, or a quarter of those voting at general meetings. Once elected to membership the annual subscription was 10s; the life subscription was £5.

As these rules illustrate, it was a selected membership, as might be expected of a largely middle-class society. In 1880 there were sixty Ordinary Members, and six Life Members.[7] This rose to seventy-five Ordinary Members, six Life Members, and two Honorary Members[8] in 1882–3. Throughout the rest of the nineteenth-century period of the Society the membership fluctuated around this size.

At the Ordinary Meetings (held twice a year) and Annual General Meetings papers were read and lectures given. These were followed by discussion amongst an audience rather larger than was usual: 'The Ordinary General Meetings of the Society shall be open to all Members and their families resident in the same house, and to all visitors and strangers introduced by a member of the Society.'[9] Along with other papers many of the lectures were published in the *Transactions of the Penzance Natural History & Antiquarian Society*; that for 1883–4 included the following reading for its members:

'Account of the Annual Excursion' (pp 307–14).

J. Ralfs, 'The Marine Algae of West Cornwall' (pp 315–30).

R. V. Tellam, 'The Marine Algae of East Cornwall' (pp 331–9).

E. D. Marquand, 'The Ichneumonidae of the Land's End District (pp 340–6).

Rev S. Rundle, 'Cornubiana' (pp 347–58).

J. B. Magor, 'The Marine Polyzoa of the Land's End District' (pp 359–68).

Rev W. S. Lach-Szyrma, 'Influence of the Fisheries Exhibition on the Fish Supply' (pp 369–71).

S. Tait, 'Carn, Marsh, Wood, and Hedgerow: A Botanical Study' (pp 372–80).

W. Curnow, 'The Sphagnums or Bog Mosses of West Cornwall' (pp 381–6).

One of Them, 'Mossists on the Tramp' (pp 387–92).

J. B. Magor, 'On the Mechanism of the Jaws of Snakes' (pp 393–7).

J. Ralfs, 'Notes on Systematic Botany' (pp 398–402).

E. D. Marquand, 'The Land and Fresh-Water Mollusca of West Cornwall' (pp 403–8).

E. Rundle, 'The Torpedo; or, Electric Ray' (pp 409–16).

A. Partaker, 'Lichen Supper' (pp 417–19).

'Additions to the Recorded Fauna and Flora of West Cornwall' (pp 420–4).

From this list it would appear that 'Natural History' studies dominated the 'Antiquarian' interests. The scholarship was often of a high standard, and illustrates well the enthusiasm of the middle classes for their intellectual pursuits.

The Museum was a centrepiece of the Society. It was held in trust for the benefit of the members.[10] All members of the Society, their families 'residing in the same house', and visitors introduced by a member had the right to visit the Museum whenever it was open.

It was in the care of four curators (secretaries), who were elected annually. The Society also allowed itself the right to appoint one sub-curator (or more) who was to be paid or otherwise recompensed for his labour on behalf of the Museum. The sub-curator held office 'during the pleasure of the Officers and Council'. Inevitably the ability of the Society to employ a professional sub-curator depended upon its financial resources, which were rarely healthy enough for such a commitment.

Those who gave specimens to the Museum, or 'parties making scientific communications to the Society' had access to the Museum, but could not introduce visitors. If the Museum had duplicate specimens the curators could exchange them with other societies or individuals. However, if a specimen had been given to the Museum with the donor's express wish that it should remain in the Society's hands, it could not, of course, be exchanged. This was the only category of specimens that might not be so disposed of.

Despite their enthusiasm for the Museum the members had to be reminded periodically of the poor condition into which it had lapsed. The President, the Rev W. S. Lach-Szyrma, in the 1880s[11] pointed out:

> You are aware the Ornithological Collection is in a sadly impoverished condition, and it is impossible to restore it without funds; and the Curators will inform you that an Entomological Cabinet is urgently needed (the present one being filled).

In the 1890s the then President, W. Bolitho, was to make a similar statement[12] on the Museum: 'The Curators report that the Museum still requires much to be done in the way of systematic arrangement before it can be regarded as either educational or scientific.'

Although it is significant that the Museum was viewed as 'educational', it was a benefit provided for a small number of people within the community. Primarily it was for the Society's members. A limited number of the members' relatives and friends could visit the Museum, but it does not seem to have been a facility to be enjoyed by the whole community on certain days, as was the case with the Royal Institution Museum in Truro.

The core of the adult education provision was in the form of lectures and meetings. These began on 12 October 1881[13] with a meeting devoted to a number of papers presented by members and afterwards discussed. It was held at Morrab House, and led to a decision to hold such gatherings monthly during the period October to March each year. The Royal Geological Society of Cornwall offered the use of the Museum for such meetings and the third was held there on 8 December 1881.[14]

These monthly meetings continued during the 1890s, with the occasional introduction of innovations to make them more interesting: 'At the March [1890] evening meeting the experiment was tried of illustrating the papers with lantern slides and the limelight (by the kindness of Mr. W. E. Baily). The result was eminently satisfactory.'[15] The early successes of the monthly meetings led to the decision in the mid-1880s to hold extra gatherings:

We have had two new departures in the past year, first, the interesting series of papers and exhibits at Morrab House . . . and, secondly, the interesting series of papers in our supplemental meeting. It is indeed something of which we (the members of the westernmost scientific society in England) may be well proud, that our ordinary course of monthly meetings has been insufficient to dispose of the number of interesting papers put at the disposal of your committee.[16]

By setting up a society which served the specialist interests found mainly amongst the prosperous middle classes, it was possible in the latter part of the nineteenth century to reap some success. Concentrating effort mainly upon one area of interest, the Penzance Natural History and Antiquarian Society found itself in a position of needing more meetings for the reading of papers and the presentation of lectures in an era when these pursuits seemed less fashionable. One of the difficulties faced by adult education in the period 1870 to 1900 within England appears to have been that of interesting an audience in a wide range of subjects. The day of the 'all round amateur' had been disappearing, to be replaced by adults with narrower vocational or hobby interests.

Research was a fundamental concern of many of the members, as might be expected of a society with such specialist interests. A review of what had been done, and that which needed to be carried out, was made in 1888 by the President:

> Botany has now been so well worked that little remains to be done in the West, but in the East of the County there is still a wide field for research, though Mr. R. V. Tellam has compiled three valuable lists of Mosses, Lichens, and Marine Algae from that division of the County. Many branches of Zoology are as yet untouched, whilst others have been only partly investigated.[17]

Just as the Penzance-based Royal Geological Society of Cornwall aimed at a comprehensive research coverage of the geology of the county, so the Natural History and Antiquarian Society hoped to do regarding its interests.

With such a strong emphasis upon natural history it was not surprising that excursions made up a significant part of the Society's educational programme. Such activities were prominent in the first year of the revised institution.[18] In 1887 these excursions were formalised into a regular monthly event, with trips of interest for the field naturalist, and to study 'ancient remains'.[19] By 1890 the summer excursions represented one of the high points of the Society's year.[20] Although these trips often had a flavour of a social event about them, they were also occasions for serious study; probably the many enthusiastic naturalists and ancient historians in the Society would not have supported the continuation of the excursions if they were only an entertainment. Although the Society had lasted only from 1862 to 1865 in its second period of life, nevertheless the annual excursions had continued until 1872.[21] They, judging by their frequency, were even more popular amongst the members after the 1880 revival.

Because of its financial difficulties the Society periodically turned to lighter fare: 'The series of entertainments given last December [1885] on behalf of the Society ... proved in every sense eminently successful, and the result financially was most gratifying.'[22]

Also popular, but with less obvious fund-raising associations, were the 'Conversazione'. As with other predominantly middle-class societies, these appeared to be organised if there was a suitable justification, ranging from the Annual Excursion in the early 1880s[23] to a three-day affair on 19–21 November 1889 'to signalize

151

the jubilee of the Society'.[24] The very doubtful claims to its being the Society's jubilee would seem to have been of little hindrance. The Central Hall was taken over in Penzance and used for the Conversazione, and for an exhibition of natural history and archaeological specimens, with lectures also as a part of the programme.

The Penzance Natural History & Antiquarian Society had a successful third revival because it fulfilled an adult educational need within the area. The middle classes in particular found great appeal in a club which specialised in hobby subjects such as natural history. Within this organisational framework the studies carried out by the members were often of a high order.

It was an institution for the middle classes and gentry. The elected Presidents were mainly Members of Parliament (eg C. C. Ross, 1880; W. C. Borlase, 1881-2; L. H. Courtney, 1888-9), or Doctors (eg J. Ralfs, 1883-4; G. B. Millett, 1886-7; W. S. Bennett, 1891-2), or other prominent members of the community such as the Rev W. S. Lach-Szyrma (1884-5, 1889-90) or the banking family the Bolithos (1885-6, 1890-1). The social structure and educational conditions of nineteenth-century Cornwall usually made separate institutions for working-class and middle-class adult education inevitable. Efforts to mix the social classes in adult education even today present great problems, and of the nineteenth century it is possible to ask if anything other than separate institutions was a feasibility. The strength of the Penzance Natural History & Antiquarian Society lay in its realistic approach to the social and educational conditions prevailing in England in the late nineteenth century. Its largely middle-class membership permitted the Society to support an extensive programme of research, excursions, papers and lectures when the working classes much preferred their own company in institutions where billiards and bagatelle were the more common pursuits. For the working-class scholar with an interest in Natural History the resources of the Society were usually available, but it would be incorrect to assume that the bulk of, say, the miners in the Penzance area were clamouring to become members and only the careful membership selection of the Society's Committee denied them access. It was the middle classes who wished to join, and the vast majority of the working classes could not have been less interested in the pursuits of the Penzance Natural History & Antiquarian Society. There is always a danger of judging the nineteenth century by what we fondly imagine to be the attitudes and conditions prevailing within our own times.

In terms of a scientific training for such middle-class amateurs the Society provided opportunities that were far from unimpressive. Not only did such local institutions bring together those interested in the field of science concerned, but permitted the concentration of precious resources. As the Penzance Society's programme demonstrates, the academic activities could prove to be rigorous, and there was a resulting accumulation of information (such as botanic surveys) that was of considerable use to the locality concerned. Before the age of full governmental provision in education, and particularly higher education, and of national surveys, the local scientific societies of nineteenth-century England had a role to fulfil that was both valid and popular.

From: *Annals of Science* (June 1971), Volume 27, no 2

Notes

Introduction

1 Cole, G. D. H. *British Trade and Industry: Past and Future* (Macmillan, 1932), 114

2 Clapham, J. H. *Economic Development of France and Germany, 1815–1914* (CUP, 1928), 285.

3 Ashworth, W. *Economic History of England, 1870–1939* (1960), 37.

4 Arnold, M. *Higher Schools and Universities in Germany*, 2nd ed (Macmillan, 1892), 21.

5 Quoted in Cardwell, D.S.L. *The Organisation of Science in England* (Heinemann, 1957), 98

6 Arnold, op cit, 83

7 Mertz, J. T. *History of European Thought*, vol I (Blackwood, 1896), 260

8 Schools Inquiry Commission *Report*, vol III (1868), 224

9 Arnold, M. *Schools and Universities on the Continent* (1868), 198

10 Department of Science and Art *Annual Report* (1863)

11 Ibid, vol XIII (1865), 12

12 Much of the work was, of course, scientific at the secondary level which later became integrated into the secondary school system as it gradually developed. It was this aspect of the instruction, no doubt, which had such strong appeal to pupil teachers, elementary and secondary school teachers and to secondary school pupils

13 Hipwell, M. E. 'A Survey of the Work of the Science Division of the Department of Science and Art, 1853–1899', M Ed thesis, University of Nottingham (1964)

14 Hipwell, op cit

15 Shadwell, A. *Industrial Efficiency* (Longmans, Green, 1906), 435

16 Extracts from 'A lecture on the Education of Civil and Mechanical Engineers in Great Britain and Abroad': being a public Inaugural Address delivered in the University of Edinburgh on Tuesday, 3rd November, 1868, by Professor Fleming Jenkyn, FRS, MICE. Taken from 'The Education and Status of Civil Engineers in the United Kingdom and Foreign Countries', Council of the Institution of Civil Engineers, 1868–70

Chapter 1: Science in the Secondary Schools

1 Ogilvie, V. *The English Public School* (Batsford, 1957), 119–20
2 Parliamentary Papers. *The Royal Commission on the Public Schools,* vol I (1864), 15
3 Parliamentary Papers. *The Royal Commission on Scientific Instruction*, Appendix I (1872), 3
4 Ibid, Appendix VIII, 32–3
5 Vide note 2, 32
6 Ibid, Appendix F, 112
7 Ibid, 39
8 Ibid, 146
9 'Darwin's Memoirs', quoted in the *Report of the Public Schools Science Masters* (1909)
10 Parliamentary Papers. *Schools Inquiry Commission Report*, vol I (1868), 229
11 Ibid, vol IX, 649
12 Ibid, vol LX, 285
13 Ibid, vol I, 33
14 Ibid, 34
15 Dean Farrow. *Fortnightly Review* (New lines), vol III, 239–40, 242
16 Vide note 3, vol III, 6th Report, 5
17 Vide note 10, 54
18 Ibid, vol IV, 585
19 Vide note 2, 56
20 Vide note 10, 56
21 Vide note 3, vol III, Appendix I, 60; vol II, 206; vol I, 67

Chapter 2: Scientific Studies in the University of Liverpool

1 Playfair, Lyon. 'The Study of Abstract Science Essential to the Progress of Industry', Introductory Lecture to the Government School of Mines (1852)
2 Muir, R. *A Plea for a University of Liverpool* (1901), 80
3 Muir, op cit, 14

Chapter 3: Technical Education: the Liverpool School of Science

1 The title was changed to the School of Science, Technology and Art in 1892, to the Central Technical College in 1935, and to the College of Technology in 1949. A central building was first provided in 1901.

2 *Report, Liverpool School of Science* (1879–80), 31
3 P 32
4 Ibid
5 P 10
6 P 16
7 Presumably Dr Carter, the chemistry teacher at the Liverpool Collegiate School
8 *Report, Liverpool School of Science* (1887–9), 46–7
9 A certificate could be won for success in a single subject. The figure represents single-subject successes
10 The centres were The Board School, Stanley Road; Liverpool College; The Royal Institution; YMCA Bootle; The British School, Mount Street; the Library; The Grammar School, Liscard; the Wesleyan School; the Brunswick School; St Peter's School, Birkenhead; St Paul's School, Birkenhead
11 The total amount of donations between 1861 and 1889 came to £1,447 10s 6d. J. Leigh Gregson, secretary of the School for many years, gave seven separate donations, and William Rathbone, MP, gave six. Other contributors included Lord Derby, A. H. Brown, MP, and W. H. Brown, MP. In fact, donations were contributed by relatively few individuals.
12 During the early 1890s the City Council felt that provision for nautical education was required and in 1892 another sub-committee of the Library, Museum and Arts Committee was constituted to organise and administer the Nautical College set up in the premises of the old Royal Institution School in Colquitt Street. The College was opened in 1892 and the staff comprised a headmaster and two assistant masters. The College was in reality an amalgam of four distinct schools catering for boys preparing to go to sea, apprentices and seamen, candidates for the Board of Trade certificate, and a higher school for officers and masters
13 Sadler, M. *Secondary Education in a Great Commercial City* (1903), 121

Chapter 4: Chemical Training in Nineteenth-century Liverpool

1 Edgeworth, R. L. *Essays on Professional Education*, 2nd ed (1812)
2 Resolutions and Reports of the Liverpool Royal Institution (1814–22)
3 Schools' Inquiry Commission *Report*, vol IV (1868), 585

4 For Queen's College, see J. T. Danson. *Report of the Council of Queen's College to the Directors of the Liverpool Institute* (1881), in the Local Record Office, Liverpool Central Library.

5 Hardie, D. W. F. 'The Muspratts and the British Chemical Industry', *Endeavour* (1955), 14, 29–33. See also the *Muspratt Papers*, Local Record Office, Liverpool Central Library

6 For Norman Tate, see W. Hewitt. *Fifty Years of the Geological Society—A Retrospect* (1910), *The Naturalist* (July 1892) and *St Stephen's Review* (30 July 1887)

7 These figures have been compiled by the authors from the Department of Science and Art's *Annual Reports*

8 For details of Norman Tate & Co, Consulting Chemists, we are indebted to Mrs M. E. Davies and Mr E. A. Hall. Mrs Davies is the widow of Edward Davies and is now in charge of the company. Mr Hall, now well into his eighties and still working in the laboratories daily, represents the end of a series of links stretching back to Norman Tate, for as a young man Mr Hall served under Joseph Davies, who in turn was trained by Norman Tate in these very laboratories

Chapter 5: The Education and Training of Engineers in Nineteenth-century Liverpool

1 *Transactions of the Polytechnic Society* (1868), 25, 33–4

2 Ibid, 34

3 Strictly speaking this was not true, most of the money being donated by Charles Beyer of Beyer & Peacock Ltd. Beyer was of Saxon origin and settled in Manchester as a manufacturer

4 *Transactions of the Polytechnic Society* (1868), 37–8

5 Ibid, 38–9

6 Ibid (1871), 36–7

7 Ibid, 39

8 It is quite clear that in making such a sweeping statement, in the eyes of the speaker the School of Science was not worthy to rank as a technical college

9 *Transactions of the Polytechnic Society* (1871), 42

10 Ibid, 43

11 Ibid, 45

12 Ibid, 46

13 Also appointed joint Borough and Water Engineer of Liverpool at the age of twenty-nine

14 In this he was quite wrong, for the figures for 1899 show that at least two-thirds of the students were artisans or apprentices, and things could not have been very different in the early years, since the school's prospectus clearly stated that this was the group of students for which it was intended

15 In 1886 the Presidential Address was 'Depression and Trade'; in 1887 'Technical Education'; in 1889 'The Education of an Engineer'; and in 1915 'The Education of a Marine Engineer'.

16 *Transactions of the Liverpool Engineering Society*, 1 (1881), 58–62

17 Ibid, 3 (1885), 170

18 Ibid, 8 (1887), 133

19 Ibid, 34 (1913), 10

20 Ibid, 6–7

21 Ibid, 8

22 Ibid, 9–10

23 Ibid, 10

24 *Journal of the Liverpool University Engineering Society*, 1 (1912), 20

Chapter 6: The Education of the Industrial Worker: the Cornish Mineworker—A Case Study

1 *Royal Cornwall Polytechnic Society Report* (1895), 20

2 *Royal Cornwall Gazette* (23 June 1837)

3 Barton, D. B. *A History of Tin Mining and Smelting in Cornwall* (Barton, Truro, 1967), 86

4 Rowe, J. 'The Rise of Foreign Competition to Cornish Tin Mining', *Royal Cornwall Polytechnic Society Report* (1965), 22

5 Ibid

6 Barton, op cit, 110, 231, 279

7 *Royal Cornwall Geological Society Transactions*, IV, 480

8 Jenkin, A. K. H. *The Cornish Miner* (Allen & Unwin, 1962), 332

9 Price, L. L. *Royal Statistical Society Proc* (1888), 15

10 Barton, op cit, 173

11 Shaw, T. *A History of Cornish Methodism* (Barton, Truro, 1967), 121

12 *The Times* (13 May 1851)

13   Prospectus of the School of Mines and of Science Applied to the Arts (1852)
14   Private communication from Sir Roderick Murchison to Lord Stanley
15   *Schools Inquiry Commission Report*, vol VII, 420
16   *Royal Institution of Cornwall Report* (1860), 8
17   *Royal Cornwall Polytechnic Society Report* (1844), 1–2
18   Ibid (1860), 16
19   The Miners' Association of Cornwall and Devonshire: *Preliminary Regulations*
20   Ibid
21   The Miners' Association of Cornwall and Devonshire Quarterly Meeting, Camborne, Thursday, 16 April 1863 (Printed by Heard & Sons, Truro, 1863)
22   Ibid, i. C. Twite was to be appointed mineral surveyor to the Government of Paraguay in 1864. R. Pearce emigrated to Denver, where he became a metallurgist connected with Colorado's largest smelter (Barton, op cit, 203)
23   Ibid, 7
24   Ibid, 8
25   Ibid
26   Ibid, 9
27   We are most grateful to Prof Charles Thomas of Exeter University for much of the material on miners' education, and on his forebear, Captain Charles Thomas
28   MACD Quarterly Meeting, op cit, 13
29   Ibid, 14
30   Ibid, 15
31   Ibid, 15
32   Ibid, 15–16. 'I do think the cost of the present working of the Miners' Association is exceedingly great for the real benefit conferred thereby on the mining population. The knowledge imparted is more showy than of real worth for practical purposes.' The words are Captain Thomas's.
33   *The Miners' Association of Cornwall and Devonshire Report* (1863), 3
34   Ibid, 8
35   Ibid, 8–9
36   Ibid, 4
37   Ibid, 5

38 Ibid, 27
39 Ibid, 6
40 Ibid, 6
41 Ibid, 7
42 Ibid, 27. The Science and Art Department's examinations came into being in 1861. Later, the Association's pupils were to take also the City and Guilds of London Institute examinations, inaugurated in 1879
43 *MACD Report* (1866), 5
44 Ibid (1867), v
45 Ibid, 4
46 Ibid, vi
47 Ibid (1868), vi
48 Ibid, 2
49 Ibid, 7
50 Ibid (1870), 5
51 Ibid (1872), 15
52 Ibid (1876), 4
53 Ibid (1878), 2–3
54 Ibid (1879), 3–4
55 Ibid (1890), 113
56 Sturt, Mary. *The Education of the People* (Routledge & Kegan Paul, 1967), 387–8
57 *MACD Report* (1891), 159
58 Ibid (1894), 276
59 Ibid (1891), 240
60 *Minutes of the Redruth Literary Institution* (3 January 1888)
61 *Royal Institution of Cornwall Journal* (1883), 254
62 *MACD Report* (1894), 276
63 Ibid (1885), 1
64 Ibid (1887), 71
65 Ibid (1894), 276
66 Ibid (1867), 4
67 Ibid (1890), 1
68 Ibid (1873), Introductory note
69 Ibid (1885), 122
70 Barton, op cit, 220

*Chapter 7: Private Enterprise and Technical Education: the Royal
Cornwall Polytechnic Society*

1 *Royal Cornwall Polytechnic Society Report* (1833), 7
2 We are much indebted to Mr E. J. Duncan of the Royal Cornwall
   Polytechnic Society for making available his notes on the Fox
   family, which formed part of a lecture given to the Society in
   1968
3 *Royal Cornwall Polytechnic Society Report* (1833), 8
4 Ibid, 4
5 Ibid, 8
6 Ibid (1834), 13
7 Ibid
8 Ibid (1833), 8
9 Ibid (1834), 16
10 Fox, W. L. *Historical Synopsis of the Royal Cornwall Polytechnic
    Society* (Falmouth, 1915), 12
11 *Royal Cornwall Polytechnic Society Report* (1842), 19–21
12 Ibid (1834), 15
13 Ibid (1866)
14 Ibid (1836)
15 Ibid (1849)
16 Ibid (1857)
17 Ibid (1887)
18 Ibid (1899)
19 Boase, F. *Modern English Biography* (Truro, 1897), 386
20 *Royal Cornwall Polytechnic Society Report* (1837), 16
21 Ibid (1846), x
22 Ibid
23 Ibid (1870), 37–44
24 Ibid (1877), 13
25 Ibid
26 Ibid (1842), xii
27 *The Athenaeum* (22 October 1877), 541–2
28 *Royal Cornwall Polytechnic Society Report* (1840), xv
29 Ibid (1871), 14
30 Ibid (1856), xxviii
31 Ibid (1849), viii
32 Ibid (1864), x–xi
33 Ibid (1867), xiii

34 Ibid (1870), 13
35 Ibid (1877), 15
36 Ibid (1884), 13, 15
37 Ibid (1889), 27
38 Ibid (1891), 2
39 Ibid (1892), 27
40 Ibid (1894), 10
41 P 15
42 *Royal Cornwall Polytechnic Society Report* (1895), 4
43 Ibid (1890), 9–10
44 Ibid (1894), 9–10
45 Ibid (1884), 55
46 Ibid (1888), 17
47 Ibid (1890), 15
48 Ibid (1898), 14
49 Ibid (1872), 24
50 Ibid (1898), 9–10
51 Ibid (1899), 8
52 Ibid (1890), 16
53 Deakin, A. N. *Some Dangers of Modern Education, Report* (1899), 32
54 *Royal Cornwall Polytechnic Society Report* (1845), xiii–xiv
55 Ibid (1841), 15
56 Ibid (1859), xii–xiii
57 Ibid (1871), 14

Chapter 8: Private Enterprise and Technical Education: the Liverpool Literary & Philosophical Society

1 Kelly, T. *A History of Adult Education* (Liverpool University Press, 1970), 105
2 Hudson, J. W. *The History of Adult Education* (Longmans, 1851), 237
3 Ibid, 113
4 Steer, F. W. *The Chichester Literary and Philosophical Society and Mechanics' Institute 1831-1924*, the Chichester Papers No 29 (Chichester Council, 1962)
5 Clark, E. K. *Leeds Philosophical and Literary Society: History of 100 years* (Jowett and Sowry, Leeds, 1924), 5–6

6 *Halifax Literary and Philosophical Society 1830–1930*, Centenary Handbook (1930).
7 *Proceedings, Liverpool Literary & Philosophical Society* (1864–5), 6
8 Ibid (1856–7), 15
9 Ibid (1897–8), xxix–xxx
10 Ibid (1844–5), xiii–xxvii
11 Ibid (1863–4), 3
12 Dr Duncan was appointed Liverpool's and England's first Medical Officer of Health
13 *Proceedings, Liverpool Literary & Philosophical Society* (1844–5), ii
14 Ibid (1850–1), Appendix, (1853–4), Appendix, (1857–8), Appendix
15 Ibid (1851–3), 2
16 Ibid (1890–1), xxxv
17 Ibid (1880–1), xxx–xxxv
18 Ibid (1896–7), xxix
19 Ibid (1863–4), 4
20 Ibid (1875–6), 1–302
21 Ibid (1884–5), xxxix
22 Ibid (1849–50), viii
23 Ibid
24 Ibid (1863–4), 5
25 Ibid (1864–5), 2
26 Ibid (1844–5), v-xii; (1857–8), 10; (1866–7), 2; (1874–5), xxii and xlii–xliii; (1882–3), xlii–xliii; (1890–1), xxxv; (1895–6), xxix; (1899–1900), xxxi
27 Ibid (1881–2), xxix; (1893–4), xxvii–xxviii; (1895–6), xxx
28 Ibid (1884–5), 1–271
29 Ibid (1865–6), 4. Fourteen Ordinary meetings seems to have been the number favoured during the latter part of the century, but extra meetings would also be arranged
30 *Proceedings, Liverpool Literary & Philosophical Society* (1881–2), xxxix–xl
31 Ibid (1885–6), xlii
32 Ibid (1846–7), 4; (1873–4), xli
33 Ibid (1848–9), iii
34 Watson, R. S. *The History of the Literary and Philosophical Society of Newcastle-upon-Tyne, 1793–1896* (1897), 339, 343, 365
35 Porter, W. S. *Sheffield Literary and Philosophical Society, A Centenary Retrospect*, The Society (1922), Appendix

36 Barnes, C. L. *The Manchester Literary and Philosophical Society*, The Society (1938), 2–7
37 *Proceedings, Liverpool Literary and Philosophical Society* (1872–3), xxxi–xxxii
38 Ibid (1860–1), 1

Chapter 9: Science and the Amateur: the Penzance Natural History & Antiquarian Society

1 *Transactions of the Penzance Natural History & Antiquarian Society*, New Series (1880), 1, 7–8. The Borough of Penzance Public Library very kindly lent us the second series of the *Transactions*, for which we are most grateful
2 *Kelly's Directory of Devonshire and Cornwall* (1883), 981
3 *Transactions* (1880), 8
4 Ibid, 8
5 *Kelly's Directory of Cornwall* (1889), 985
6 *Transactions* (1880), 1, 9
7 Ibid, 5–6
8 Ibid (1883–4), 191–2
9 Ibid, 1, 11
10 Ibid, 11–12
11 Ibid (1884–5), 2, 7
12 Ibid (1890–91), 3, 198
13 Ibid (1881–2), 83
14 Ibid, 177
15 Ibid (1889–90), 3, 106
16 Ibid (1885–6), 2, 127
17 Ibid (1887–8), 2, 307
18 Ibid (1880), 1, 8
19 Ibid (1887–8), 2, 307
20 Ibid (1889–90), 3, 106
21 Ibid (1889–90), 3, 105
22 Ibid (1885–6), 2, 117
23 Ibid (1881–2), 1, 170
24 Ibid (1889–90), 3, 181

Acknowledgements

In the writing of these essays we received generous help from many sources. In particular we would like to mention the advice and suggestions of Professor Emeritus John Allaway and Professor H. A. Jones of the University of Leicester, Professor Charles Thomas of the University of Exeter, and Professor Thomas Kelly, Dr John Rowe, and J. J. Bagley of the University of Liverpool. Our apologies to those to whom we are also indebted, but which space does not permit us to mention.

As with all such writings we owe a considerable debt of thanks to a number of librarians and archivists. John Vaughan, Tutor-Librarian of the School of Education at the University of Liverpool, and Peter Rowley, Institute of Extension Studies Librarian at the University of Liverpool, were, as always, an endless source of assistance and advice. N. G. Carrick of Liverpool's Local Records Office, and the Staff of the Cornwall County Records Office at Truro were of great support. Our demands on other libraries and institutions were legion, and our progress would not have been possible without such kindnesses and encouragement.

Lastly we would like to thank the Editors and Publishers of the *Annals of Science*, the *History of Education Society Bulletin*, *Paedagogica Historica*, and *The Vocational Aspect of Education* for permission to reproduce these essays.

G.W.R.
M.D.S.

Index